D0957715

HELP!
MY KID WANTS TO

BECOME A
YOUTUBER

MICHAEL BUCKLEY &
JESSE MALHOTRA

COPYRIGHT

Cover Design: Michelle Grierson

Interior & Back Cover Design: Jennifer Stimson

Editing: Maggie McReynolds

Authors' photo courtesy of Robin Thompson

ADVANCE PRAISE

From Fellow YouTube Stars

"This book is funny, inspirational, and filled with great tips. If it wasn't for Buck's advice and support in the beginning of my YouTube career, I wouldn't be where I am today."

Shane Dawson, *New York Times* best-selling author of *I Hate Myselfie* and *It Gets Worse*

"Buck is a true innovator, groundbreaker, and gladiator for the new era of digital content creation. He taught me the value of taking risks to make my voice heard in a sea of noise (both on YouTube and at karaoke night)."

Grace Helbig, *New York Times* best-selling author of *Grace's Guide* and *Grace & Style*

"I have never met anyone more absolutely, 100% themselves than Michael Buckley. Which, in my opinion, is so important for kids to witness. Michael is a round off, backhand spring of a human. And his writing is no different."

Mamrie Hart, *New York Times* best-selling author of *You Deserve a Drink*

DEDICATION

For my mother, who always wanted me to be a star but passed away before YouTube was even a thing. She is loving this!

TABLE OF CONTENTS

FOREWORD

People ask me all the time how to become a YouTuber, and it's simple: you make an account and upload that first video. But I can't guarantee that it won't suck. In fact, it will be far from perfect. And I can assure you, it will be appalling to see your mannerisms or to hear your voice for the first time like this. But I can absolutely promise you this: it will be exhilarating. That's how you know you're a YouTuber.

When I began in 2007, it was intoxicating. I wanted to make a video about everything that happened to me. I day-dreamed about skits and collaborations and rants that I could film; I began to film in my free time and watched any YouTuber I could find. Because I started before the platform really boomed, my outlook on YouTube was never about being the most viewed or most subscribed, but instead, making content that I loved and sharing that with whoever wanted to watch. Sure, I wanted views and sub-scribers, but back then, everything felt fresh, and because nobody was really profiting off of the platform yet, goals centered around creativity, not marketability. Of course at the start, there were YouTubers who had found huge success, but like any celebrity, almost all of them seemed unreachable – that is, except one: Michael Buckley.

Back when I was first starting out, Michael Buckley was my pop culture news. Like most people my age, I lost interest in TV and major news outlets for my celebrity gossip fix, and instead, turned to salacious bloggers and vloggers for a more personal take on the happenings of Hollywood. I didn't want the manufactured rumors and boring predictable takes during the daily news cycle, I wanted an honest and hilarious stance – something that could only be found on YouTube. Michael Buckley had created a platform for himself that not only offered that, but gave it in a way that had never been done before. He found his own voice on YouTube, making content that he cared about and that made him happy.

I loved Buck's videos – I watched him every day, and gasped and cackled at his hilarious, no-holds-barred approach to celebrity news. Instead of going to frat parties, I stayed in to watch his livestreams, where he offered advice and community to tens of thousands of people all around the world. I found my first sense of digital community with him and his viewers, and I looked up to him as a pioneer in the digital realm.

The best part about Michael Buckley was, and remains to this day, his passion for creation, and his earnest paternal instincts within the YouTube community. He was the first YouTuber to ever reply to me, something that made me jump around my dorm room, screaming. He was the first YouTuber I ever collaborated with, even when he had 100x the amount of subscribers as me – to him, that didn't matter – he just wanted to make fun stuff and help amplify the voices of everyone in the community. His love for YouTube comes from his love for people, and his desire for everyone to succeed. During his time on YouTube, he's redefined success in Hollywood, proving that you don't even need to relocate to Hollywood to take over the industry. He proves that success comes not necessarily from breaking records or blazing new trails (though he's done both for almost a decade), but from following your own path and doing what makes you happy. He's done all of this, while remaining honest, hilarious, and compassionate. I'm proud to say he's inspired me for a decade, and I'm honored to call him a true friend.

This book is perfect for anyone who aspires to follow their own path – and to learn from someone who, to this day, consistently redefines what it means to be a digital entertainer. It's not about how to be famous, what's the secret ingredient to a viral video, or any of that garbage. It's about how to navigate this intimidating world, and how to have the most fun doing it. If you've always dreamed of being a YouTuber, this is for you. If you have a friend or family member who aspires to make it happen, this is for you. If you have a simple curiosity about the world of YouTube, this is for you. If you want to hear from the man who was there for the first wave of success, and has stuck around through a decade of digital ups and downs within the industry, this is for you.

YouTube has never been about one singular experience – there are so many ways to be a YouTuber. My faith in Michael's ability to reach any type of creator lies in his ties to all kinds of creators in the community – you simply can't find a successful YouTuber who wouldn't list Michael among their all-time favorite creators, and there's a reason for that. He cares about this community, whether you have 1,000,000 subscribers, or just one, and is eager to help you in whatever ways he can.

I was recently asked in an interview what my "big break" was. I thought for a moment, thinking about accomplishments or milestones in my almost decade-long career on YouTube. Being a YouTuber has opened so many doors for so many creators – thanks to their audiences, they're able to expand into the world of books, movies, TV shows, hosting opportunities, product lines, collaborations with politicians or celebrities – the list goes on. Having dabbled in about a million side projects while still uploading every week to my YouTube channel, I thought about how many of those opportunities changed my life, but nothing compared to my biggest break of all: uploading my first video. Because that actually was my big break. And the best part about it? Anyone can do that – and if you need help, Michael Buckley is here to guide you.

Tyler Oakley
New York Times Best-Selling Author
December 2016

INTRODUCTION

Hello, New Best Friend!

If you have seen one of my videos, I'm hoping you read that in my voice with great enthusiasm!

Welcome to my first book! OMG! I wrote a book! I have been meaning to write a book for years. I am so glad *this* is the book I am writing. Years ago, publishers would reach out to me asking me to write a book about "How to Be a YouTube Star." That book really didn't interest me. A) I was one of the only YouTube stars. Why would I want to tell everyone else how to do this? B) To be honest, it sounded like a boring book to write. So technical!

Over the past year, I teamed up with a childhood friend, Angela, and her son, Jesse, to create a business teaching kids how to be YouTube stars. This was way more fun than writing some kind of manual. It is a series of video tutorials, much more my speed.

Those video tutorials cover the HOW TO, but something was missing, and that is the WHY.

Why would someone want to be a YouTube star? Specifically, why would your kid want to be a YouTube star?

WHY WOULD YOU WANT TO LET THEM?

Suddenly this is a very interesting book for me to write! Even though I was working with Angela's son, I still felt a disconnect. She didn't "get" YouTube and why her son was so obsessed with it. This book is intended to bridge the gap between you, your child, and their face buried in their screen watching videos.

I wanted to write this book for parents or anyone who wants to help understand YouTube better or help the kid in their life develop their channel. The kids are all in! They love YouTube! They don't watch TV the way we did. Everything is "on demand" or on YouTube. They look at their favorite YouTube stars like Markiplier and Rowan Atwood the way we looked at rock stars and movie stars. These are the biggest role models and heroes in their lives.

I want to make sure you understand the power of YouTube. YouTube changes lives! YouTube saves lives! I am not being dramatic. YouTubers get emails from all over the world and their fans often tell them the same things:

"You inspired me to work hard and achieve my dreams!"

"Seeing you live your best life makes me want to live my best life!"

"You saved my life!"

Go look at the comments on the videos your kids are watching. They have tens of thousands of comments all basically saying *you make my life so much better!*

You may feel you have lost your kids to these online stars. I prefer to think they are co-parenting with you!

Lots of parents want to limit their kid's screen time, but I say LET THAT SCREEN TIME BE LEARN TIME!

Every kid I talk to wants to start their own YouTube channel, but they are not sure how to begin. Or they just make silly, unedited videos with their friends – but then they are not sure how to get more people to see their videos or take their content to the next level.

I wrote this book to give you some tips to empower your kids to be the best YouTubers they can be! There is a lot to learn and you don't have to be an expert in everything – **LET ME DO THAT FOR YOU!**

It is important for you to know some basics to help them set up their channel and be aware of their online safety as well. I know you have concerns about privacy and online bullies. These are things we will discuss in upcoming chapters.

I promise you that – regardless of whether your kid makes money doing this or becomes a YouTube celebrity with people waiting four hours to meet them at VidCon – from **IDEA to UPLOAD,** they will learn amazing like skills that will transfer to anything they do in life. Networking! Collaboration! Self-confidence!

I will also share stories of kids who grew up making videos. What have they learned? Would they do it all over again? What do they wish they knew before they hit upload? These are huge YouTube stars who have gotten 50 and 100 million views on individual videos!

Jesse will chime in at the end of every chapter with his unique take on becoming a YouTuber, how his relationship changed with his mom, and what it's been like to work with me. His words and his opinions are all his own!

I am not going to make you a YouTube expert, but hopefully I will make you an expert in empowering your kid to be the best version of themselves they can on YouTube – either as a fan or a creator.

So excited to share one of the great loves of my life with you – YouTube.

"I DON'T GET YOUTUBE"

I get it. You "don't get it." You don't understand why your kid would rather watch YouTube videos than do pretty much anything else in the world. There they are, at the dinner table, in the car, on your family vacation, *sitting right next to you*, and they are more connected to that freaking website than you.

You have just made your famous pot roast but you have to wait to eat because the world needs to stop. They have checked their subscription feed and –

"Oh my God, Mom! Stampy Cat has a new video!"

"Pewdiepie just got this new game and broke some score! Or got some level or blah blah gaming!"

"Rowan Atwood just filled his entire living room with balls! MOM! HIS WHOLE LIVING ROOM IS A BALLPIT!"

You look at your child as they tell you this.

Are they speaking in English?

Did a cat make a video?

What is a Pewdiepie? Are they living in some alternative universe? Are they making this all up? Don't they wanna go see the new Tom Hanks movie with you? You would even let them watch *The Walking Dead* with you at this point! They would rather watch YouTube than connect with you.

THIS SUCKS!

I know you made an attempt to understand. Once. You probably watched for 10 seconds but were annoyed by the YouTuber's strangely pitched, frantic voice and didn't see the entertainment or inspiration your kid's favorite YouTuber was providing.

WHAT THE HELL?

Have they brainwashed my kid? Did this YouTuber make a video called "How to Piss Your Parents Off" and your kid is now following through with this YouTuber's dastardly plot to annoy you? Maybe. I'm kidding. Okay, seriously, search for that video. I am sure there are a few of them out there somewhere. But I also bet they finish with a lesson on how you should be nice to your parents and not piss them off and they just wanted to grab your attention with a catchy title! I know my YouTube peers; they are a good bunch and really have your kid's best intentions at heart. It does take a little research and open-mindedness to fully grasp this, but after being in the space for 10 years, I assure you that YouTubers, for the most part, are awesome. Your kids have good taste in entertainment!

That said, I totally understand your concern. Your kid is obsessed with YouTube, and you are annoyed and nervous about the relationship he/she has with their screen – and, more specifically, this odd person who is making videos about God knows what. Sex? Drugs? The new MacBook Pro? (The latter is most likely.)

In a way, this is your fault. You gave them the screen, didn't you? How could going outside and playing in the dirt compare to Markiplier's new video? It can't. You feel guilty. You have created this monster! Good luck.

And you just know it's about to get worse. They've started uploading their *own* videos. Oh, no! They want to make YouTube videos like their favorite stars. This is terrifying for parents. It's scary! It's dangerous! It's a time-sucking waste of effort.

Actually, it is exciting, safe, and a *great* use of time once you understand it from their viewpoint – and that is why I am here to help you!

My friend Angela reached out to me last summer. Angela was actually already on my vision board as someone I admired; I saw her doing powerful, life-changing things with her business. I wasn't sure exactly why I was putting her on my vision board, but I knew I wanted to keep tabs on her and be motivated by her and hopefully work together on something. I didn't know what, but the Universe did.

Angela sent me a message saying she had a 10-year-old son named Jesse who loved YouTube, spent all of his time watching YouTube, and had recently started making some vlogs (video blogs) and gaming videos. No plan. Just plopped some videos online, like many kids do.

For a year, Jesse had been nagging Angela to help launch his channel and help him figure some of the stuff that he couldn't figure out on his own. Mom, of course, was very busy and felt guilty that she kept putting him off. But like most parents, she didn't really get it, either. So over the next year, she and Jesse grew apart because she didn't have an interest in his primary interest. And it's not like she didn't care. It truly was just a foreign land. Angela used Facebook and it was a big part of her business, but she couldn't wrap her brain around this YouTube thing.

She is not alone. This is totally new territory for parents over the past decade. If your kid expresses interest in baseball, you sign them up for Little League. This makes sense to you. If your kid likes art, you can take them to the parks and rec department for a drawing class. Duh. But when a kid loves YouTube and wants to become a content creator, most parents scratch their heads, or scoff, or make excuses and redirect, or even shame the kid for having such a lazy hobby. Right?

Also, you don't want your kid to do it on their own and do it wrong. Then it becomes some mess you have to clean up. So you don't have time to help them, you don't understand how to help them, and now you and your kid are truly disconnected. This is sad and painful for you. I get it.

Then Angela remembered she had a friend from middle school who was a successful YouTuber. Oh, hello, Universe and Vision Board in action! Angela hired me to mentor Jesse for four hours a week via Skype. I gave Jesse the one-on-one attention he needed to start building his YouTube channel properly.

Wait. A 10-year-old is going to have their own YouTube channel? Not only is this scary, but doesn't this reflect poorly on me as a parent? Here are some of the concerns you might have:

- **Why can't I figure YouTube out on my own? – I must have failed as a parent!** You are busy running your own business and your household. You don't have the time to spend on this or the skills needed to be a YouTuber. And let's be honest, your kid is probably more tech-savvy than you are! That is why I am here, and that is why you have this book – to help you help your kid.

- **Won't other parents judge me for hiring someone to work with my child on silly YouTube stuff?** Again, if your child likes horses, you hire a riding coach. This is the same thing. But it's 2017! Your kid loves YouTube. You hire a YouTube coach. You are not a bad mom for doing this. You are a great mom for doing this, and this is the best gift you can give your kid this year!

- **It's not healthy for my kid to have so much screen time!** I politely disagree. Your kid is learning and investing and plotting the rest of their life when they are online. They are being inspired to create! YouTube is art to them. They are going to a museum and studying the great works of art for their generation! *Screen time is learn time!*

- **Making videos is a waste of time and won't lead to anything!** Not every kid in the school play ends up on Broadway. I am here to tell you that the life skills, the organizational skills, and the self-confidence your kids learn on YouTube are invaluable, regardless of what they do with the rest of their lives. You know this in your gut; you just need someone to remind you so when anyone questions your parenting, you can reply with, "I love that my kid is doing something they love. This is their passion and I am nurturing it." BOOM! Drops mic. P.S. Aren't other parents the worst? Can't you lift each other up rather than judge each other? I should make a YouTube video called "OTHER PARENTS ARE THE WORST." HA!

- **Isn't it unsafe to post videos online where creepy people will have access to my kid?** There is a whole chapter in this book on Internet safety. Of course you need to be involved and monitoring their YouTube use. You need to be doing this anyway, even if they are not making videos yet, whether they have an account or don't have an account. You need to be checking what they are doing online. In terms of posting videos, I will make you feel a lot better about this. I will help you know what to look for and how to determine when to engage and when to just block and ignore. Is there danger? Sure. There is also danger in football and soccer and figure skating. You learn what the dangers are, and you help your kid understand how to play smart.

Any other fears or mental blocks holding you back? Feel free to contact me. Let me tweet you through it! The moment you stop fighting your kid on this and start embracing it, you will have a much happier household. And yes, your kid should eat dinner and then watch YouTube, but once you've read this book, you will be more sympathetic to their desperation to *watch it right now*. After all, MY FAVORITE YOUTUBER JUST POSTED IT AND I NEED TO LEAVE A COMMENT SO THEY SEE ME!

By the end of this book, you are going to understand your kid a lot better and have a better relationship with them. You might even make a video together? Let them suggest that, though. Don't try to get into the act too soon! I can suggest some great family challenge and tag-style videos when we work together.

Angela and Jesse are closer than ever now! They are connecting in new and wonderful ways. Jesse has a vision board and big plans for his channel and beyond. Mom and son went to a popular gamer convention, MineCon, last year. It was so worth it! Perfect mother/son bonding!

Angela saw firsthand how Jesse's face lit up as he met some of his favorite YouTubers. She delighted in his self-confidence when he told other creators he had a channel and he asked if he could interview them on camera.

Her 10-year-old knows how to network and make contacts! He knows you need to collaborate to grow your business, so he is doing just that. And Mom doesn't have to feel guilty anymore. She has given her son the tools that empower him to create and prosper.

She "gets it." She sees the value in her son watching YouTube. She sees the great joy and pride he has in his channel. He is learning new skills. He is improving his on-camera persona. He is learning how to set goals, problem-solve, and strategize. I give him homework that is fun for him. YouTube is his hobby, his passion, his creative outlet, and his greatest joy. What could be better for you as a parent than seeing your kid aspiring and succeeding at their favorite thing? I can't wait to see what he does next.

I am excited to see what your child will do with their YouTube channel! Let's do this!

Is your kid ready to get started on his or her own YouTube channel? I have a special offer just for my readers – seven free lessons from my BecomeAYouTuber video course, made especially for your child to follow! Just go to **www.becomeayoutuber.tv/readeroffer** to get started.

From Jesse: What Your Kid Wants You to Know About YouTube

I like YouTube because it makes me feel like I'm doing what the YouTuber is doing in the video. Most YouTube stars are doing things instead of telling stories like on TV. Watching YouTube is more exciting because you know it's not make-believe, and it's something you could actually do if you wanted to try it. YouTube stars can become your idols and your heroes, but characters on a show can't be your idols or heroes because they are made-up characters – you can meet the actor, but not the character. YouTubers can do meet-and-greets and you can meet the actual person you see on YouTube.

When my parents don't want me watching YouTube, it makes me feel upset and frustrated, because there is always something new to watch. There are a lot of YouTubers and each of them posts on different days/weeks and at different times. There is always a YouTuber posting a video you can watch! When one of my parents says, "Go outside," I don't want to.

One thing I would like for parents to do is get to know who our favorite YouTubers are and what that YouTuber's upload schedule is, so they aren't asking us to do chores or go outside right when a new video shows up. If it was the Super Bowl or even a favorite TV show, everyone would know what time that was on, but most parents don't even think to ask when our favorite YouTubers are uploading.

That's really important to a kid. Also when a kid finds a new YouTuber they like, there are usually a lot of videos to catch up on. It's like finding a new TV show to watch on Netflix.

For example, there's this channel called "What's Inside" I really like. When I first started watching, I would scroll down to the bottom and there were like 75 videos I want to catch up on. Think about it. If you liked a show, would you want to skip ahead three seasons in and find there's a new character and three other characters are dead? That's what it's like when you find a new YouTuber you like. You don't want to skip ahead.

I get excited by all the choices there are on YouTube. Regular TV doesn't seem like it has enough on it to me. I think regular TV doesn't have as much variety in types of shows.

DanTDM is one my favorite YouTubers. I had the opportunity to meet him at an event where a lot of the kids came with their parents. Dan said he loves it when parents watch videos with their kids and when they're both fans. When he said this, I realized I want my parents to watch my favorite YouTubers, too. I don't want my parents stuck watching videos they don't get, don't like, or think are weird, but I'd love to share some of my favorite channels with them because it's something I'm interested in. I want my parents to like what I like so we can spend more time together.

YouTube is unique because it makes me feel like I am with the person whose channel it is. I really wish more parents got this because it's something I feel like they are missing out on.

It was cool to work with Michael because even though he mostly watches different shows than I do, he really gets what is so special and unique about YouTube. In this book, Michael is going to tell you, as a parent, what you need to know to help your kid get started on YouTube like I did. For my part, I'll be helping you understand your kid's thoughts and feelings about all of this so you get maximum value from the book. Basically, you can pretend Michael is you and I'm your kid!

When I was writing this book, my mom and I got to talk a lot about my opinions about YouTube, and I liked sharing these ideas with her. We are learning a lot about perspective at school, and I hope my part of this book helps you understand your kid's perspective on YouTube better. Maybe it will even spark some conversations you and your kid can have about YouTube and making videos.

CHAPTER 2

MY YOUTUBE STORY

I started making YouTube videos in the summer of 2006. Until that point, I had no idea what YouTube was. I had a public access show in my hometown of Wallingford, Connecticut, and my cousin took clips of the show and put them on this thing called YouTube. I thought it was strange. Why would I want strangers all over the world watching my hilarious videos? Shouldn't they be just for the people of Wallingford? I found the whole thing odd. If someone found out that I was posting videos online, they would make a strange face, wonder aloud why I would do that, and assume I was in the adult entertainment industry or something they deemed shady.

When I started, I didn't even have high-speed Internet or my own YouTube account. My cousin would upload my videos on his channel. I remember that when I first got 100 views, I thought, "Oh my God! I am famous!" At first, I would get an average of eight comments on each video. Six would be along the lines of "Die!" or "You suck!" Welcome to the world of Internet discourse in 2006! I did what any rational person would do. I created an account called "BuckFan1." (Apparently "BuckFan" was taken?) I would leave myself comments like, "You are so funny, Buck!" or, "Keep making videos!" I was always my own biggest fan!

Eventually I made a channel called Peron75, named for my love of Eva Peron and the musical *Evita*, as well as for 1975, the year I was born. Please note: *This is a terrible YouTube channel name!* Unless I was making a channel about the Perons or the number 75, it makes no sense. Cryptic YouTube channel names should be avoided. Presently I have two YouTube channels: BuckHollywood and NewMichaelBuckley. These are great YouTube names!

People often ask me how to become a YouTube star. I tell them the truth: it takes a little luck and a whole lot of hard work. My first few years, I was working 40 hours a week at an office job doing lots of filing, lots of spreadsheets, and even grabbing my boss coffee while also spending 50 hours a week writing, editing, filming, and promoting my videos simply because I loved it. I had well over 100 videos before I started getting big view counts.

I felt so empowered by the site. I wasn't waiting in line going to auditions and hoping to be cast in someone else's project. I was creating my own project. I was feeling bored and unsatisfied by my job and had always thought I should be a talk show host or a comedian. Suddenly I was both! I loved creating the *What the Buck Show* from scratch. It was definitely one of the first, if not *the* first, of its kind on YouTube: a scripted, one-man show with news and humor in the style of SNL's "Weekend Update" or "The Soup" on E. It was five to nine minutes of me talking about hot topics and making jokes about celebrities and the ridiculous things they seemed to be doing. It was a hit!

My first year and a half was very strategic. I was the first YouTuber to ask for ratings and comments. The week I did this, I had the four highest rated, most commented videos on the site. My Wikipedia page cites this. I looked at the camera and asked for the people watching to rate the video five stars (now you press the thumbs up/like button instead), and to please leave a comment. I made opening credits that were a call to action to Rate/Comment/Subscribe! A week later, all the other YouTubers were doing the same thing and realizing the effectiveness of self-promotion and engagement with the audience. As an OG YouTuber, I take great pride in this legacy.

I also put myself on a schedule. I posted every weekday around 4 pm ET. At this time, the other top YouTubers were posting once a month or whenever they felt like it. I developed a programming schedule that made me accountable, and the audience grew because I was delivering content on a consistent basis. Again, once I started doing this, others saw the value in it and did the same.

I had no idea where it would take me or if it would lead to anything. But I fell madly in love with making videos, watching other people's videos, leaving comments to see if a famous YouTuber would notice me, and meeting fellow creators from all over the country and making videos together.

YouTube became a great love of my life.

When I started in 2006, it wasn't possible to make money. It certainly wasn't possible to make a living making online videos. This changed quickly when YouTube figured out a revenue-sharing program for creators like me who were getting millions of views per month. Yes, you can make money from YouTube. But hold that thought; we'll talk about it later in the book.

In the summer of 2007, I was invited into the YouTube Partnership program. YouTube called me. I was at work. I went to the parking lot to take the call, as I didn't want my boss to know what I was up to. I cried – and filmed a reaction video right then in the parking lot. Hey, I am a YouTuber! That's what we do!

I had no idea what it meant or would mean, but I was so proud. There were about 75 of us. Now there are tens of thousands of YouTube partners, but it still feels nice to have been in that first group. By the summer of 2008, I was making a lot more on YouTube than I was at my office day job, so on September 12, 2008, I left my office job and become a full-time YouTuber! At that time, I also had an HBO development deal, which didn't lead to a series because the HBO Lab I was working with got bought out by Break.com, but they paid me a year-long salary for basically a month's worth of work. I also had a contract with Sony for an online show based on TV shows I loved as a kid, which ran for a year and got me a live-streaming deal with BlogTV (now YouNow) to broadcast live three hours a week. It was a very exciting time in my life, and I jumped in with no fear! *The New York Post* came and took photos and ran a great story about me. "He is leaving his day job and all his dreams are coming true!"

There was no business model for this career that I had stumbled into and yet also manifested and worked my butt off for. I was negotiating brand deals with major clients to make sponsored videos for five figures. It was nuts! Some of these one-off videos paid me more than my day job had paid me for a year. I had to figure it all out as I went. I helped other YouTubers launch their careers by giving them guidance and promotion.

I was flown to London by YouTube to give a speech and teach many of the media companies in the UK, including BBC America, how to use YouTube effectively. None of them understood the value of YouTube. They saw it as a threat to their TV audiences. They didn't understand that kids were watching bootleg copies of it on YouTube anyway, so they might as well get on board and create a proper channel.

In many ways, I was the poster child for YouTube success in the early years. *The New York Times* ran a photo of me on the cover in December of 2008 with the headline, "YouTube Videos Pull In Real Money." People all over the world saw this and thought, "If this guy can do it, I can do it!" When I go to YouTube conferences now, many very famous YouTubers mention that article and tell me it inspired them to pursue becoming full-time content creators. It feels great to know that I empowered people this way.

Over the years, my star continued to rise. I was cranking out five to eight videos a week, and I was frequently on TV doing interviews and talks about my online success. I felt like I was on a hamster wheel and I wasn't sure if I should hop off before I was thrown off!

I loved being a YouTuber, but it was challenging to have something that started as a hobby morph into my job. Over the years, I burned out many times, and began to resent the site and long for the old days when it was simpler. I loved it. I hated it. I hated myself for hating it. Where was my gratitude for this amazing site that had changed my life so beautifully?

But I kept making videos and doing lots of mental gymnastics to keep my head in the game. And yes, YouTube is a game! It is, in many ways, a sport that you need to learn to play, mentally and physically. I was like the guy who wins the Super Bowl three times, but can't seem to retire. I still loved the game. I just loved it differently. I was beginning to feel like I didn't really love being a YouTube star anymore, and that I would rather help others be YouTube stars.

I wasn't sure how I would do this, but I began plotting – or at least visualizing. When I would go to YouTube conferences, I began shifting my focus. I started mentoring up-and-coming channel creators and helping them set goals.

By 2014, I felt a major shift in my purpose on the site and my overall passions. I was no longer as interested in pop culture, which was what the *What the Buck Show* was based on and what most of my revenue was largely contingent upon. I felt very locked into the format I had created for myself, and it grew increasingly difficult to maintain this online persona – BuckHollywood, who knew what all the celebrities were up to and made jokes and commentary about them.

Over the next year, I got divorced and then two of my five dogs died; it was a lot to process and a lot of change. I had to give serious thought to the rest of my life and what I wanted to accomplish on and off YouTube. I was overdue for a real heart-to-heart with myself.

Teaching and coaching had long been things I thought I would be doing. I bought a life coach certification book in 1999, and was sure I would be a life coach. It was like I had wanted to be a coach for years, but then became a YouTube celebrity and forgot.

Over the years, I had an advice series on YouTube called *Dear Buck*, where I would give viewers advice on how to deal with their parents, dating, overcoming fears, coming out of the closet, setting goals, being their best self – these ended up being my favorite videos to make. When I watch those videos now, I see my true and ideal self doing my best work and fulfilling my greater purpose on the site. When people would meet me and tell me *What the Buck* was funny, I would always say, "Have you seen *Dear Buck*? I think I'm kinda funny, but really good at advice. Watch those!" HA!

So in 2016, with zero regrets, I stepped aside from my BuckHollywood persona and focused on being my true, authentic self on camera and off. I started creating more advice/self-help videos and became a certified life coach. Finally! Yay! One of my certifications is in YouTube coaching! It's amazing to work with up-and-coming YouTubers and also some of my peers who need help avoiding YouTube burnout, balancing online and offline life, and strategizing how to best use the platform they have.

I still do an episode of *What the Buck* a few times a month, and now every time is amazing because it's no longer my everyday thing. I have embraced the persona as a small part of who I am online instead of my entire identity online. I feel balanced online and offline. At last!

I let my content shift with my interests rather than being stuck doing what had been expected of me for 10 years. It has been very gratifying and incredibly liberating to combine my love of YouTube and coaching.

It was the summer of 2016 when I started mentoring Angela's 10-year-old YouTuber, Jesse. This was huge! Totally life-changing! And totally manifested! I have always been a big fan of *The Secret* and the power of visualizing! Remember, earlier in the year I had put Angela on my vision board to manifest working together somehow.

We worked on strategic planning, good behavior on the site, programming schedules, and setting goals. I saw YouTube through the eyes of a kid, and I fell in love with it all over again. I realized this was part of my greater purpose; this was exactly what I should be doing to pay it forward out of respect for my love of the site.

Then Jesse and I put together our training program called **BecomeAYouTuber.TV** It was the first business for both of us! A ten-year-old and a forty-year-old – better late than never! The program is made up of 15 video training modules that teach kids 8-14 how to start and grow their YouTube channel using all the tips and tricks I have learned over the past 10 years. Of course, I hope you will get it for your kid and want to work with me one-on-one the way Jesse did!

The program is the how-to all those publishers wanted me to deliver years ago. This book, however, gives you the why: why you should actually *want* your kid to be a YouTuber. They may or may not become a YouTube star, but they will have learned amazing life skills along the way. They will go off into the world and be able to do anything with great confidence and purpose.

YouTube is magical! I know it. Your kid knows it. And I hope that by the end of this book, you know it!

From Jesse: What Your Kid Wants You to Know About Michael

If you're thinking about having your kid work with Michael, you should know that Michael is really funny and energetic. If your kid is really committed to getting their channel going and if they are patient and funny, they will love working with him.

But this only applies if your kid isn't going to be mean to him! I'd say be nice to him and listen to him. Do what he says, and it will make the whole thing even better.

Working with Michael is fun. I liked that he got to teach me because I got to grow faster on YouTube and I got that boost I needed. I think he helped me the most with keeping my channel looking nice so it looked populated and well-designed.

It's hard to stick with the schedule that he gave me, but I know that the more I stick with the schedule, the more successful I will be. Michael kept me moving forward even when I was busy with camp and school.

If you start uploading more, you will start gaining subscribers. If you leave a single comment, people might see it. But if you leave a bunch of them, you will start to meet people.

CHAPTER 3

GETTING STARTED ON YOUTUBE

Starting your journey into the world of YouTube with your kid doesn't have to be overwhelming. Let's ease into it.

First, let's eliminate the "I don't get it" argument. It is dismissive and not productive. Let's seek to understand! The best way to do it? Create your own YouTube channel! You heard me. Well, create your own YouTube account, at least. You probably already have one and might not know it.

If you have a Gmail address, you have a YouTube account. If you are logged into your Google account and you click on YouTube, you will likely notice you are signed in there as well and ready to like/comment/subscribe just like your kid has been doing.

I know many parents feel overwhelmed when they first look at the YouTube home page. Where should you look first? The trending videos? Your subscription feed? The videos YouTube is suggesting based on what you watched recently? *Sneaky YouTube! How did they know I was watching cat fail videos? UGH!*

Don't let that freak you out. YouTube knows you better than you think!

My recommendation is that you get cozy with your laptop or desktop while you're getting used to YouTube. You can, of course, watch on your phone like many kids enjoy doing, but I think navigating the site on your computer is easier to start. I am old like you, so I get it! HA! And if you are watching on the mobile app, you might get a text or a Facebook notification or something popping up and distracting you, so let's just commit to 30 minutes to an hour of simply clicking around and getting better acquainted with YouTube.

It is very easy to fall down the rabbit hole with videos, so stay aware, and save them for another time. I have gone to watch just one music video and then found myself three hours later sitting there wondering how I ended up watching a full Celine Dion concert and every TV interview with Cher. It happens! Easily.

In any case, look around. Go to the search bar on top. You are searching on YouTube, not in your browser address bar. (Just making sure we are on the same page.)

You will find that most of your favorite TV shows have YouTube channels. You can watch all of Ellen DeGeneres' shows on YouTube in the morning before they even air on TV! That is pretty cool. SNL posts all their skits on YouTube! Many of your favorite cooking shows have great behind-the-scenes content on YouTube! If you don't have cable, some of the cable news shows stream live on YouTube! When you think about how you consume your favorite entertainment, YouTube is every bit the provider that Netflix, Hulu, and Amazon Prime are. It is amazing! How could you have stayed away for so long?

EVERYTHING IS ON YOUTUBE!

I enjoy watching gymnastics and figure skating from the 1980s and 90s. I watch old tennis matches. Jimmy Connors' 1991 US Open? I could watch that every day for inspiration! TED Talks! How to get a squirrel out of your fireplace? A mash-up of your favorite sitcom's opening credits over all nine seasons? YES, PLEASE! You name it, it's on YouTube. So feel free to search for anything you want!

I learn so much by watching how-to videos on YouTube. I've learned how to edit videos, how to set up my lighting, how to change a headlight in my car, how to set up my coffee maker, how to get a squirrel out of my fireplace. (I wasn't kidding about that one!) My point is, anything you enjoy is likely on YouTube. It's a treasure trove of content!

As a YouTuber, I also spend time watching my friends and favorite YouTubers like Phil DeFranco, Shay Carl, Tyler Oakley, Mamrie Hart, Shane Dawson, Hannah Hart, Grace Helbig, The Fine Brothers, and The VlogBrothers. Oh, have you seen *Sci Show*? They teach you about science! Believe me, you can find great videos about math and science and geography and graphic design – anything. I think it is so cool to have all this at our fingertips!

By all means, watch things you enjoy. But I also want to encourage you to subscribe to a handful of the creators you know your kid watches. Regardless of whether you end up enjoying these videos, you are doing your research and monitoring their YouTube habits, as you should.

There are many daily family vloggers who you might fall in love with and enjoy watching as a family. There are fitness vloggers you can exercise with every day. I quit the gym and now use YouTube videos to exercise.

Make some playlists of things you enjoy! This is a fun and easy way to participate on YouTube. When you see videos you like, you can add them to a playlist so it is easy to watch them again and find them on your channel, just like a watchlist you'd make in Netflix. This playlist lives on your channel. You can make it private so only you can see it, or public so if someone clicks on your page, they can see it – totally up to you.

- I have made playlists for:

- Christmas karaoke music for holiday parties!

- Ab exercises!

- Walking meditations and pep talks!

- My favorite figure skating programs of all time!

- Funny interviews where celebrities say crazy things!

- Broadway shows (totally bootleg and illegal, but pretty much any Broadway show you want to watch is up on YouTube – and it *not* illegal for you to add to your playlist!)

Leave some comments on videos you like – relevant comments, of course; we want to model appropriate commenting for our kids! If you start leaving nasty comments on political videos, don't be surprised if your kid thinks it is okay for them to leave nasty comments on videos. Be mindful of your contributions to the site.

When you scroll through the comments, you'll see that they're posted in chronological order so the most recent comments rise to the top. Also the most- liked comments rise to the top too. So if 1000 people like your great comment, it will stay at the top of the video and people will see it.

When you see a video with lots of likes, you can tell it is popular and well-appreciated. If you see a video with more dislikes than likes, the video probably has some racist, sexist, or otherwise controversial message. Lots of times you will see lots of dislikes on political videos from Fox News or CNN. That is just the way YouTube and the United States are in 2017, so don't overthink the dislikes on those types of videos. But if you notice your kid is watching a video with lots of dislikes, I recommend watching the video yourself to make sure he isn't getting a message that you don't like. These are just some things to think about as you click around the site.

Okay, so you have spent some time on YouTube. Once you have an account and you have left a comment or liked a video – TA DAH! You are a YouTuber! Regardless of whether you're making content or not, you are watching content, so you are part of the YouTube Community! Welcome!

Now that you've tiptoed in on your own and you have a little more understanding of how YouTube works, it's time to break it to your kid that you are in their world, too. HA!

You can let them catch you watching their favorite YouTuber. That would be fun! Or you can sit them down for a heart-to-heart about wanting to understand their love of YouTube better. Whichever you think will be more effective or amuse you more. You are in charge!

Tell your kid you want to watch together, invite them to show you their favorite two or three videos, and ask them afterwards what they liked most about them. Treat this as a learning exercise for you. Use this time to learn about their tastes and see their world through their eyes.

Don't ask with a judgmental tone, like: "What the heck do you possibly like about this?" Instead, note something in the video that catches your eye and say, "I liked this part. What did you think about this _____?" Again, just seek to understand. Remember that YouTube is, for many parents like you, what rock music was to your grandparents. Loud! Annoying! Incomprehensible! But you don't have to be your grandparents. You can bridge the gap!

If they flip out and say something like they don't want you to watch because it's their thing, not yours, then that is where the parent comes in and tells them that if you can't watch, they can't watch, plain and simple. But hopefully they will think it is cool that you're enthused about what they are enthused about. Let's hope for a full-circle enthusiastic moment!

And believe me, when your kid asks you to pay to take them to VidCon or MineCon or AnyCon next year – and they will – they will want you to be well-versed in this stuff! It makes it easier for both of you. I love seeing kids at conferences with their parents. I love when a 12-year-old tells me they watch my videos and, and then their mother or father who is my age or younger tells me they watch, too. That is awesome!

So now you are on the road to being fans together – if not of the same YouTubers, at least of the same platform! We have some common ground.

They probably already have an account, but if they don't, you can help them set up their Google account. Tell them it's important to be logged in so they can like, comment, and engage with the other users, especially if they want to build their own channel. This is how most YouTubers start:

as fans, active members who comment and share posts of their favorite videos.

I have a whole training video in my program that teaches kids how to become what I call Curators of Content. It teaches kids how to make playlists, format their page, and give people a reason to click on it even if kids haven't uploaded any videos yet. You can find it at BecomeAYouTuber.TV.

Ask your kid if they like or dislike particular videos. Ask them what types of comments they tend to leave on videos. Who do they subscribe to and why do they subscribe to them? What types of videos do they make? They will love that you have taken an interest.

I had Jesse set up his page so that the Recent Activities tab shows – you can easily do this, too. That way, Angela can see what videos he has watched and liked because the activity shows up on his feed. I recommend you do so as well in the interests of safety and knowing what your kid is interested in.

So there you go: you and your kid are both YouTubers! And if they are like Jesse, or my nieces and nephews, or pretty much any kid I talk to, they want to make videos of their own. Let's give them some tools and guidance to get the most out of it.

Exciting stuff ahead in the next chapter! But I am glad you are on board and ready to help support them!

Is your kid ready to get started on his or her own YouTube channel? I have a special offer just for my readers – seven free lessons from my BecomeAYouTuber video course, made especially for your child to follow! Just go to **www.becomeayoutuber.tv/readeroffer** to get started.

Homework for both of you: Ask your kid to like and comment on five videos over the next day; you will do the same. Then tomorrow you can look at each other's Recent Activities and see what videos you each liked and talk about it.

From Jesse: What Your Kid Wants You to Know About Getting Started

I was surprised that logging into YouTube was hard or over-whelming for parents. When I log in, I just look at the buttons and what they say and, depending on what they are, I click on them. It's obvious for me what to do next, so it didn't occur to me it wasn't obvious to you. One thing you might want to do is ask your kid to teach you. If my mom or dad asked me, it would make me feel good because it would show they were interested and wanted to learn more about what I like.

When I first started using YouTube, I subscribed to channels, liked some videos and commented on others, and made playlists, all before I ever made a video myself. All of this made me feel more a part of the community.

Even if this seems hard for you, I think you should try it and see how it makes you feel that way, too.

Sometimes, my parents see me watching YouTube and say, "Who's that? He's so annoying!" or "What are you listening to?!?" That makes me feel upset and frustrated. I put on headphones and sort of check out of the conversation, because I figure I'm just going to keep annoying them if I don't. But it makes me sad when they don't appreciate what I watch.

I love Michael's idea in this chapter of asking your kid about their favorite YouTubers when it's a good time for you, so you're not just reacting to some noise that distracted you from a phone call or conversation. I love the idea of being able to show you some videos that I think you would like from some of my favorite YouTubers. It's totally different than being yelled at for forgetting headphones on a long car ride!

I can understand why you might not want to watch my shows. If my Mom or Dad asked me to watch something like an old TV show from the 80s, I would say, "No way, that's too old." I hate old stuff. So if there is something you have always wanted your kid to see and they haven't been interested, here is your chance! If you watch my stuff, I will watch your stuff.

Maybe you don't want to get started. Maybe it feels too hard to you, kind of like homework sometimes feels too hard to me. I hope you'll get started anyway. Reading about how parents feel about their kids' interests makes me wonder if my kids will someday have their own version of YouTube that I won't like. I hope I will at least take some time to try to understand it.

CHAPTER 4

MAKING YOUTUBE VIDEOS

Okay! So your kid wants to be a YouTube star, or, at the very least, make their own videos and see where it takes them. How do we do that? More importantly, how do we help nurture that?

First off: know that they don't need much, at least not in the beginning. A simple phone or tablet comes with a great camera these days, and many are pre-loaded with simple editing tools. My point is that you don't have to rush out and buy a $2,000 camera before your kid can start making videos. A camera phone, a laptop camera, or an affordable small camera like a Canon PowerShot will all do just fine. Natural lighting works great, too! And if your kid wants to do gaming videos, there is software they can download to record directly off their computer to capture their game play.

Pro-tip alert: if you look in the description of your kid's favorite YouTubers' videos, you'll see that many list the equipment used. Again, you don't need this now, but it can be good to know for future reference. Many pro-Tubers use the same camera and lighting kit.

There is a whole tutorial on **BecomeAYouTuber.TV** that talks about cameras and other equipment you can find at various price points. My lesson here for you is that if your kid is telling you they need all this fancy stuff to start, you can tell them I said no, they do not, and to just get to work with that they have. As they start to grow, we can talk about upgrading their equipment.

When I left the public access studio to film full-time at home, I did buy a decent camera since I was making money – but I also saved money by buying a pair of work lights from Home Depot and a $6 piece of fabric from Walmart that I used as a green screen (most YouTubers are not using green screens, but I figured it out!). I also watched an eight-minute video on YouTube that taught me how to properly light my green screen and "chroma key" (a special effects technique for making a composite image from two sources) the background. Did I mention how wonderful YouTube is for educating people of all ages? *Screen Time Is Learn Time!*

One of the first things I do with clients is a Passion Test. You can do this, too. Ask your kids to write down a list of things they are passionate about. Things they *love*! Then review the list with them and discuss how, together, you can turn what they love into a YouTube video.

There is an audience for *everything* on YouTube!

Something to watch out for: settling for copying other YouTubers. In some ways, imitation is fine! Your kid loves these YouTubers and is drawing inspiration from them. Jennifer Nettles likely wanted to be Reba McEntire, who wanted to be Dolly Parton, who wanted to be Loretta Lynn. New content creators rarely have to reinvent the wheel. They don't need to come up with some style of video or format that does not yet exist. Your kid should focus on making the types of videos they love the most.

That said, *they should not copy another YouTuber simply to get views.* This is not a good long-term strategy. If your kid doesn't love and believe in the videos and is just trying to "get famous" or "get lots of views," it will be a long and depressing road to stardom! And the audience is smart – they can tell when someone is just going for the views and not really passionate about the content they are creating.

So my advice to you as a YouTube parent is help your kid focus on making videos they truly love and are excited to share with the world.

Many, many kids come up to me at conferences or email me and want advice on making videos. I always tell them the same thing: JUST START. Make a video! You will figure it out as you go – what works, what doesn't work. You won't know until you start posting, so get to it!

Tell your kids that their videos do not have to be perfect. They never have to be perfect. That is not what we are going for. Their videos will develop as they develop.

Just remember, most YouTubers look back on their first videos and cringe. Do not be afraid!

Let's go over some different types of videos your kid can make. These are just a few examples; the possibilities are endless!

FIRST-PERSON VLOGGING

Vlogging is what most kids like, and if I had to guess the type of video your kid would choose to make, it would be this.

The YouTuber is talking directly to the camera. You share your thoughts. You share your opinions. You share silly stories about what happened at school (without violating the privacy of other students or teachers, of course). Basically, this is just turning on the camera and talking! You can take your camera on the go and splice some footage in to make the video more visually interesting, but first-person vlogging is a great option because it helps you with public speaking and helps you form your opinions as well as express them in a concise manner. This style of video is very popular, and the audience really connects with them. I always tell kids that the greatest gift they can give the world is to be themselves – and that is what first-person vlogging is. Now, your kids can certainly adopt a "character" and do first-person vlogging as that character, but trust BuckHollywood, that can be exhausting over time.

I've spoken to a lot of YouTubers who want me to tell kids to make sure they develop a YouTube persona they are going to want to and be able to sustain. So be yourself – although you generally make these videos with a somewhat more enthusiastic, more opinionated, and heightened version of yourself.

UNBOXING VIDEOS

Lots of kids love these! They get a toy or a tech product and they take it out of the box and play with it while they explain the features. My nieces and nephew watch these videos for hours! This is one of those formats that you might scratch your head about and wonder how people could watch this. They do!

LET'S PLAY GAMES VIDEOS

Gaming is huge on YouTube. Minecraft! Call of Duty! Grand Theft Auto! The Sims! People love playing games and recording it, and your kids love watching it! Sometimes these YouTubers are pro-gamers who are very good at playing. Other times, the gamers are failing but doing hilarious commentary as they play. This is another genre your kid is likely to fall into.

COMEDY/SKETCHES

One of the first big breakout stars was Fred, a fictional young boy played by Lucas Cruikshank. Lucas and two other kids had a sketch comedy channel. It was just the three of these kids being silly, but it took off and became very popular. (More about Lucas in the next chapter.) So this can be a challenging type of video to pull off. You may watch and find yourself thinking, "Oh, gosh. My kid is *so* not funny," but you never know down the road, so if sketch comedy is of interest to your kid, tell them to go for it! Look at Miranda Sings, who now has a show on Netflix based on her YouTube sketches!

HAUL VIDEOS

These are popular with lifestyle and beauty vloggers. Often, they will do a back-to-school haul and show the back-to-school clothes they have purchased. Or they will go to the dollar store and show all the funny things they got for a dollar! These are easy videos to make, but because you have to buy things, they can be expensive.

CHALLENGE VIDEOS

This is a great way to jump on a trend and get views. Be careful though! Some of these are scary. You might have seen a variation of these on TV where people are eating raw cinnamon or putting a condom over their heads. So if your kid wants to do a challenge video, just make sure you know what they are doing!

TAG VIDEOS

Tag videos are great for young YouTubers and super easy. You can actually Google search "YouTube tag videos," and a long list will pop up that includes all the questions! These videos are basically Q & As: the YouTuber answers the questions and then tags other members of the community to make the same videos! Fun! Easy!

HOW-TO VIDEOS

If your kid is really good at something, I would encourage them to make tutorials. If they are great at a sport, for example, there are other kids who are going to love watching a fellow kid give them tips. If they are great at crafting, cooking, organization, math, singing, dancing, making animal noises, anything – for all of these, either a tutorial video or a straight-up "this is my talent" video works great!

REACTION VIDEOS

Lots of kids do this. Meaning, they react to news, to TV shows, to other YouTube videos. I have definitely made plenty of these videos – reacting to the Presidential election, the Casey Anthony verdict, a YouTube prank video that freaked me out, the Olympics, the Academy Awards – lots of my *What the Buck* shows were basically reaction videos to current events. These are easy, very searchable, and very accessible videos.

Just be aware that there are many styles of YouTube videos. It's your kid's job to figure out the format that will serve their goals and their creative passions. You can help with this – and I can certainly help with this when we work together. Reach out to me at **BecomeAYouTuber.TV.**

I want to caution you about intentionally setting out to make a viral video. Most of us YouTubers hate that term. When we first started working with marketing companies, they would ask for a viral video and we would have to break it to them that this is not really how it all works.

Things tend to go viral for strange reasons that are hard to predict. Viral videos are great to submit to America's Home Videos or to share on Facebook to make someone laugh. They are not a great long-term strategy for building a successful YouTube channel. So please resist the urge to have your kid hit you in the crotch, or do something silly and or dangerous to try to gain traction. *Do the work!*

CASE study   *David After Dentist:* A Cautionary Tale for Parents

In January of 2009, a viral star was born when David Devore posted a video of his son, who had just been to the dentist and had a hilarious reaction to the anesthesia. Here is an interview with David about their story, and an update on what David is up to now.

David After Dentist has over 130 million views! What do you think made the video go viral?

First, it's just funny to see a kid going through that and expressing himself like an adult. I also believe it was timing. YouTube was still new and anything remotely funny was bound to be a big hit. It was also easier to be found on YouTube back then.

The video was beloved but did you face criticism from either strangers or anyone in real life for posting a video of your kid on the Internet?

Yes, I did, but not much. I took offense at first, but quickly realized those who really cared about David would reach out to me privately. The rest were trying to bring attention to themselves. They ranged from commenters to reporters like Bill O'Reilly. They were just taking advantage of our viral video by criticizing it.

In a 2015 Today Show interview, David says he thought it was funny and he was not mad that you posted it. Did he think it was funny at the time? What did he make of the initial attention? Was he reading comments?

He doesn't remember much, but did find it funny that night when we watched it. He enjoyed the attention and experiences but is a regular kid when it comes down to it, and would rather hang with friends and play sports. I honestly don't think he read one comment! We really kept him from that and censored them in the early days. My wife would review them each night while watching TV.

Clearly you had no idea when you posted it what would happen! Your channel name is booba1234. What does this name even mean?

HA! Funny story. That is my nickname from my wife. I am southern and she is Spanish. One day we were taking with a friend about the southern nickname Bubba. We wondered what that would translate to in Spanish. That's when BOOBA was created.

How did you monetize the video?

We started with a partner program, and then licensing has become the larger source of revenue recently. Merchandise was ok, but as you can imagine it is short-lived. Having said that, the recent election cycle has people all, "Is This Real Life?" about Donald Trump, so we came up with a cool design for it that we are selling.

You posted a follow-up video that did very well. Did you think you were going to build a channel of David doing viral things? In general, it is hard to build a channel following a viral video. Did you feel that way? You have posted videos on and off since then. Did you have any posting strategy?

It is very hard. Even if you want to be creative with something tied to it or totally new, people can be very critical of you – maybe more critical of that than of me posting in the first place. They said I should just drop it and stop trying to milk it. I have to admit this really weighed on me when I had ideas. What helped was that David wasn't really interested back then in doing things, so there was my answer. If he had been all excited about it and wanted to build on it, I hope that I would have ignored the haters and did it anyway just for fun. We recently started posting again. My younger son is very funny. Our biggest laughs have come from just being in the car (ironic, isn't it?), so I just set up a camera on the way to school and edit it into something I hope is entertaining.

Is there a YouTube future for you or David? Where would you like to see the channel go in the future?

As he gets older, it will be up to him. In two years, he will be in college and very busy with that, so I am not really sure.

What did you learn from the experience as a parent and as a businessperson?

We have always been about the experiences and making memories from our video going viral, so you just enjoy it as much you we can. On the business side, take what comes your way and don't take it for granted. Oh, and put aside some for taxes, that bit us hard one year!

Any advice for parents who want to post YouTube videos of their kids and how to make it a good experience for the family?

Just make sure it is something they want to do and enjoy. Don't do it just for money or fame. Be original with what you create. Remember also that these kids eventually grow up and may have different opinions on it as they get older. We have had to go through this several times. David is now 16 and has asked us for a heads-up when we are telling people about the video. He doesn't like surprises, especially those that focus attention on him. Another down-the-road decision is, "When do we transfer the whole thing over to him to let him handle it?" Those are the long-term questions I think we will see as we make our way down the long road of Internet fame and celebrity.

Any tips for parents of kids who want to be YouTube stars?

Just proceed cautiously and make sure to communicate as a family. Be careful of third-party managers. I recommend managing it yourselves as long as you can, especially with younger kids. Seems things start to get crazy the more people are involved and the farther away it gets from the parents' control.

HOW TO MAKE MONEY ON YOUTUBE

Let's finish this chapter by talking about how you make money on YouTube. Maybe you even skipped to this section! This is the number one thing most people want to know when they ask me about YouTube.

The simple answer is that Google runs ads at the beginning of YouTube videos, and you, the YouTuber, share the revenue. Also, you can make money from branded content. Much of the time, your kid's favorite gamers are playing games they were paid lots of money to play and promote. When a YouTuber recommends you download a book from Audible.com, it is lovely that they are encouraging you to read – but they are often being paid thousands of dollars for that recommendation.

The Federal Trade Commission (FTC) has gotten very strict about the guidelines for sponsored videos, so YouTubers must disclose in their video's description that this is paid-for post. If you see a hashtag such as #Ad or #Spon, that means it's a sponsored video.

I told you at the beginning of the book that I was one of the first YouTube partners. It was very flattering at the time. Now anyone who wants to can be a YouTube partner. Once you sign up for a Google Account, under account settings, you can click "Enable Monetization" and link a Google AdSense account. Once your account has $100 in it, you will receive a payout.

You make money based on the number of views your video gets. In simple terms, it is safe to guess that if your videos are getting millions of views, you are making thousands of dollars. If your videos are getting thousands of views, you are getting hundreds of dollars. This varies greatly based on the cost per thousand impressions (CPM), meaning the advertiser is paying for the number of times the ad is shown, not the clicks it receives.

Some YouTubers have a $2-$6 CPM. Some have a $20+ CPM. It depends on what category their videos fall into. It also depends on whether they are being sold as part of a package YouTube has put together for an advertiser. Oftentimes, a YouTuber will be part of an MCN (Multi-Channel Network), and they might guarantee you a certain CPM. Examples of MCNs are Fullscreen, Maker, Big Frame, BroadbandTV, and Style Haul.

If you are part of an MCN, they will pay you directly. There are pros and cons to joining an MCN. I would not worry about that right now at the beginning. Just keep it in mind for the future. Please reach out to me directly at **BecomeAYouTuber.TV** if you would like some guidance on this. As part of my coaching process, I can put you in touch with people who are signed with different networks to give you some insight into their experiences.

YouTubers also make money selling merchandise such as T-shirts, posters, and laptop stickers. Many also have popular podcasts on iTunes and SoundCloud and have had great success bringing in sponsor dollars. Many do live shows for their fans and make lots of money selling out performing arts centers. The YouTube community has several *New York Times* best-selling authors now! Grace Helbig, Shane Dawson, Tyler Oakley, Mamrie Hart, Hannah Hart, Rosanna Pansino, and countless others have converted their YouTube audience into book sales. This is just to let you know the sky is the limit, and that YouTube is often just one piece of the puzzle for our leading YouTube celebrities!

Now, of course they do it for the joy and the passion and the love of making videos – but who doesn't want to make money doing what they love? YouTubers are truly living the dream. No wonder your kid wants to be just like them!

Is your kid ready to get started on his or her own YouTube channel? I have a special offer just for my readers – seven free lessons from my BecomeAYouTuber video course, made especially for your child to follow! Just go to **www.becomeayoutuber.tv/readeroffer** to get started.

 ## From Jesse: What Your Kid Wants You to Know About YouTube Videos

I mostly watch gaming, vlogs, how-to, and challenge videos. These types of videos are the ones I consider fun and cool, so they are the most interesting to me. The ones that I watch are the same as the ones I make, maybe because I understand how they work or understand the style better because I am making them. Here's what's weird. As a parent, you probably think I'm watching gaming videos to teach me how to play the game. Kind of, but not really. I watch gaming videos because I like watching someone else play the game, and it helps me think about how I can make a video playing a game.

My sister, Sofia, does cartwheels and she always wants us to watch. So we do, and I clap with everyone else even though it gets boring seeing her do it like 100 billion times. I want people to watch me do my stuff, too, and that's what gaming videos are like. It's a lot more fun to post a gaming video and have people watch than to ask your parents to watch you play in real life. No one wants to do that when they're tired and just want to relax.

I think that it would be great to make money off my own videos, but making videos is not a chore to me. It's really fun, and so if I get money or not, it really doesn't matter. It's all about participating and making something that others will enjoy – and that I will enjoy when I make it. That said, I think it's great that people can make money from something that they are passionate about.

I also like to buy merchandise from YouTubers I follow because it shows other people who I like to watch. It's a good conversation starter at school and at conventions. So if I wear my favorite YouTuber's logo on my shirt, I get to meet people who also like them, and we can start conversations about something we both know about and love watching. Also I think I look great with a fantastic logo on my clothes. You can also get lunchboxes and backpacks with YouTuber logos, and other people will compliment you on them. It's a great way to make new friends.

Buying your kid merchandise from a YouTuber they love is a way to show them you are paying attention and support their interests. The kids will love getting accessories from their favorite YouTubers and, with most types of merchandise, it's stuff that kids need anyway – clothes, school stuff, small toys. So it's a good thing for both parents and kids... everyone's happy!

CHAPTER 5

MY KID'S FIRST VIDEO

Your kid has now made a video or a few videos! YAY! Now what?

In this chapter, I am going to help you reconcile your kid's expectations with reality in a loving and encouraging way.

So your kid has posted a video – and guess what? They were contacted by *The Today Show* for making such an amazing video and they get to sit with Kathie Lee and Hoda and drink non-alcoholic wine and talk about how their life has changed since making this amazing video. Then CNN will call and they will be talking to Anderson Cooper about their masterpiece! Oh, and the next issue of *Variety* will feature your child on the cover with the headline, "THE NEXT BIG THING ON YOUTUBE!"

Actually, this is probably not going to happen. Your kid might be discouraged about the lack of pomp and circumstance. They have been so excited to be a YouTube star for so long and they finally made a video! Again, I say YAY! But we need to prepare them for how it is probably really going to go.

They probably got 10 views, eight of which were them. They probably got one like, which was also them, and zero comments. WHAT THE BUCK HAPPENED?

As I have told you, when I started I got very few views, I rated my own videos, and I left nice comments for myself. I was also 31 years old and thought it was hilarious that I was doing this.

This is when you have to break it to your kid how difficult it is to actually build a following and a subscriber base on YouTube. It's also when you will get a good sense of whether they are doing it for the wrong reasons. If they want to quit right away, that's fine. This is probably not for them. Tell them you are proud they made a video to see what it was like, and now they can go back to being a fan vs. a creator/fan. Nothing lost. If they still want to make videos, bravo! Your child is making videos for the right reasons and is already demonstrating resiliency and stick-to-itiveness!

The process is what needs to be fun at this point. The celebration is not about view counts and likes yet. The effort should be rewarded. And how cool and brave that they have put themselves out there! Wow – that's incredible!

Now, if they get mean comments, I will tell you how to handle that in Chapter 8. For now, they have not gotten any comments, and they won't until they start actively promoting their video. You can certainly post it on your Facebook, Twitter, or other platforms if they want you to share it with your family and friends. Ask them what they want and let them decide.

Jesse made a vision board for his YouTube channel with "ten thousand subscribers" and a picture of the YouTube gold play button that YouTube sends you when you hit one million subscribers. Those are wonderful goals, but we also remained realistic. When he hit 50 subscribers, he made a video to celebrate and thank his viewers. When he hit 100 subscribers, he did a giveaway to honor this milestone! It's the little victories along the way that are going to keep kids motivated and focused.

Here are some examples of milestones to aspire to and celebrate with your kid as they build their social media empire.

- 10 likes on a video, 20 likes – all the way up to 100 likes! (Have your kid make a chart to keep track.)

- 5 comments on a video, 10 comments, etc.

- First 10 subscribers! First 25! First 50! First 100! And on and on!

As your kid surpasses these goals, encourage them to set new ones, like:

- A famous YouTuber likes one of my videos.

- A famous YouTuber replied to a comment on my video.

- A famous YouTuber tweeted me back or liked my tweet!

Interacting with other YouTubers and getting them to notice your channel is not only exciting for your kid, it's good networking! (More on this in Chapter 6.)

Don't forget they are kids – make the milestones fun and reaching them a game! Caution: only do this if your child has expressed a desire to achieve higher numbers and build a following. If they have told you they're just trying to have fun, back off – there's no need to push it. But if they are serious about growing their channel, help them set small goals.

In the last chapter, my main piece of general advice for your kids was to *just start*. The next step? *Try different things!* Don't be afraid to change formats. That was my biggest problem for years. I got stuck doing the same type of program and was nervous about changing it. I didn't want to take the risk or make the effort to figure out something else, even though I was burned out and had begun to dread creating my videos. What if I changed and people were mad? What if people unsubscribed? Luckily, I am now fearless and I don't worry about anything. It took me years, but I finally realized that you can't please everyone. And you certainly can't please all strangers on the Internet who watch your videos. I love the videos I post, and I hope others do as well.

If your kid has a format they love, it's going well, and they're motivated, great! But during these first few months, it's not a terrible thing even if they seem directionless with their style of video and their channel is a total potluck.

Sometimes you have to try a few different things until something sticks, meaning that the style of video works for you and lands well with the audience. Ideally, it is both!

If you've been exploring YouTube, you've likely seen the Fine Brothers. For years, they were making wonderful videos in a variety of styles. Then they launched a show called *Kids React*™, and BOOM! That was their turning point; they found a winning format! Their channel caught on, and now they have billions of views. It is the best feeling as a YouTuber when you find something that works, is easy to produce, and will never get old. People will always love watching kids reacting to things – it is so simple and yet genius! I love the Fine Brothers and highly recommend their channel. This is totally something you can watch as a family, too!

Lots of YouTubers have similar stories of trying multiple things before they found their sweet spot. Jesse interviewed EvanEraTV and learned that just a few years ago, he was making all kinds of videos – if you look at his channel, you'll see that there is no rhyme or reason to the content. There are videos with less than 1000 views that have nothing to do with his current videos. Now he gets hundreds of thousands, even millions of views per video on his *Magic Trick* and *Magic Prank* videos. That's not what he started out doing. He figured it out as he went!

One of the challenges your kid might face is one that all YouTubers struggle with to some degree: making videos you love to create vs. the videos your audience wants to see.

It takes a while to find the balance. A lot of times, a YouTuber will make three videos a week. Here is an example of a suggested schedule:

- Monday – create and post a video in a format your kid enjoys making.

- Wednesday – create and post a different format your kid enjoys making with a call to action: "What do you guys want to see from me on Saturday's video?" So, they are asking their audience to basically help them create their next video. Taking suggestions from your audience in the comment section is a popular and powerful YouTube tool.

- Saturday – use those audience suggestions to create and post a new video.

It is also fun and easy to do Q & A videos. Your kid can ask the audience to leave comments with questions that they can answer next time. They can also do this on Twitter and any other social media platforms they use. I am sure you will notice that a lot of their favorite YouTubers do this.

I hope you found these tips helpful. I just want you to feel like you understand a bit more what goes into all this and point your kids in the right direction when they need it.

Lucas Cruikshank, the Original YouTube Child Star

One of the first breakout celebrities was a young boy from Nebraska who became a YouTube star before there was such a thing. Here's an interview with him.

Why did you start uploading videos on YouTube? What different types of videos did you post early on?

I grew up in a big, crazy family and my older sisters were always making stupid, silly videos with my mom's giant camcorder, so video-making was something I've always been around. Around the age of 12, I wanted to be able to store my homemade videos somewhere, and I somehow came across YouTube. I literally thought it was just a place to store your videos, so I was surprised when random people from all over the world starting watching. I think my first official YouTube video was a clip of my cat with absolutely no audio filmed from my crappy Walmart webcam. I also posted a lot of skits, parodies, and extremely cringey dance videos that I prayed nobody from my middle school would ever see (they did).

Did your parents know? What did they think?

My mom eventually found out, and at first she was hesitant. She was scared strangers would find out where we lived and kill us, which luckily hasn't happened yet. She knew how much I enjoyed making wacky videos, so she let me do it.

What were some of the first comments you remember? How did you handle negative comments?

I'm pretty sure every comment I received in the beginning was something along the lines of "you suck" or "please die," which, thank god, I found hysterical. I found it so funny that some stranger somewhere else on the planet was so offended by my innocent videos that they felt the need to comment horrible things. Eventually, though, actual supporters started watching my videos, and I always try to focus on people's comments who are on my side. When my character "FRED" really blew up, negative comments seemed to dominate my videos, and for a while it really did affect me. I never liked sports or really anything that boys my age seemed to enjoy, so YouTube was the one thing I felt like I was good at, and the massive amount of hate comments did bring me down. I actually almost quit doing YouTube when I was 16, and a group of guys from my high school made a hate Facebook group about me. My older sisters found it, and when I looked at it I saw the names of some people who I thought were my friends. It sucked, and I was so humiliated that I honestly thought there was no way I'd be able to continue to make videos. It was one thing to see negative comments from strangers, but to see people from my own school joining in made it real to me. Thank God I have a supportive family who helped me get through all of that, or I probably would've actually quit and ended up being, like, a miserable Walmart greeter somewhere.

What was your inspiration for the "FRED" character? Did you have any idea it would be so big? It must have been nuts to be getting 10, 20, 50 million views per episode! You had Super Bowl numbers on your series!

People always ask me what inspired "FRED," and to be completely honest, I have no idea. By the time I created Fred, I'd been making videos pretty regularly, so it was just another video to me. I was just being silly in my basement with a witch hat on, and decided to make a video parodying six-year-olds. I thought it was hilarious, so I was excited that people online wanted me to keep going with it.

You had a lot of opportunities early on before people knew anything could come of being on YouTube. How did you navigate the business part of it?

I navigated the business side of things, well, horribly. I said yes to everything because I was so excited people wanted to work with me, but that lead to me being way too bogged down, especially while still attending regular school every day. It was super fun though, and my mom helped me keep up with things, but I'm pretty sure there's an entire Fred joke book out there somewhere that I've never once read and am not sure if I was paid for. I also almost went on a Fred lip-synching Christmas song tour – I thank the Universe every day for not letting that actually go through.

Was it difficult to leave your character "Fred" behind, or were you ready for other things?

It wasn't difficult. I never wanted Fred to last more than a year, and it ended up continuing throughout all my teen years. I've always loved comedy and creating new things, so being boxed into one character was frustrating at times. I wanted to try new things, but my management and people I was working with only seemed to care about FRED.

You went from YouTube to TV and film and then came back to YouTube. What do you love about YouTube after all this time and what motivates you to continue to make content online?

Yeah, it's crazy. I love YouTube because you can wake up, make something, and show it to people all within 12 hours. I feel like I have such a connection with my audience, and the platform is constantly changing, so it keeps things interesting.

What life skills have you learned from being on YouTube all these years?

I've learned to adapt to new things and to find humor in eight-year-olds telling me to "get a life."

What is your best piece of advice to a young person just creating their channel and starting to make videos?

To have fun! I had so much fun with my channel when I first started, and I wasn't scheming to get more sub-scribers and views. I feel like with YouTube, if you focus on that side of things, it can get exhausting really quick. Focus on your content and don't give up – it took me many months before anyone cared about anything I was uploading, but at least I knew my mom and my one fan, Greg, were watching! Plus, if you're having fun, who cares if anyone is watching.

From Jesse: What Your Kid Wants You to Know About Their Channel

I set my goals by thinking about what number of subscribers would be important to me: 100, 1000, 10,000, a million. I started by doubling what I already had with a big goal of 10x my current number, and then I put that on a vision board. A vision board is something that helps you think about all the things you might want over the next year. When I made my vision board, my mom was with me, and it was something fun we did together.

To make a vision board, you put all sorts of pictures of the things you want most onto a big sheet of paper and hang it in your wall. That way, whenever you look up, you see the things you want the most and it helps you actually achieve them because they are with you all the time.

Sitting down with your kid and creating a vision board with them helps you understand what you kid wants and what is important to them. It gives the parents a chance to know what to do to help their kid achieve the goals that they have for what they enjoy in life. It's such a useful tool to see your kid's dreams on their wall.

My mom helps authors write their books. One of her authors is a lady named Cassie Parks, who writes about something called the law of attraction. I asked Cassie to help me attract my goals. One of my goals was to meet DanTDM, one of my favorite YouTubers. Cassie asked me to close my eyes and envision what I wanted to happen. Once I pictured everything, she had me identify how I felt, and then I took the energy and visualized compacting it into an orb and putting it in my heart. Then I repeated it a couple of times. She told me not to do it too much, and so I didn't. Then, it happened just like I imagined it!

Setting goals for their YouTube channel is a great way for kids to learn about things like the law of attraction. I use my vision board and what Cassie taught me for things besides my YouTube channel, like if there is a test I want to get a good grade on.

My biggest milestone was reaching 200 subscribers. I got there in less than three months, which I was really happy about. I started with no one, so if I think about how many people I know, getting to 200 is a really big achievement. I hit this milestone when I was at a convention, so I did a giveaway of all the extra things I had left over from my convention goodie bag to my subscribers. I worked out all the extra stuff I had left over and used a random-name-picker website. The winner got all the leftovers from the goodie bag. It was pretty much free for me, and they were super happy.

Hitting 1000 and 5000 subscribers will be big milestones for me. I think I have another giveaway planned for one of them, and the other will be a big special challenge. I'm still working on it right now, but it's gonna be great. You should ask your kid what their favorite celebration videos are from their favorite YouTubers.

CHAPTER 6

FROM IDEA TO UPLOAD: GAINING LIFE SKILLS

YouTube teaches kids lots of skills that are transferable to their offline and future selves.

The first skill Jesse and I worked on was **building consistency and sticking to a schedule**. He was posting occasionally and randomly, whenever he felt like making a video. This is fine if that is what your kid wants to do, but Jesse wants to grow his channel, be a YouTube star, and get invited to conventions as a Featured Creator, so he needed to get more focused and create an upload schedule.

Your audience likes to know when they will see you again so that, at the end of your video, they're not left wondering what happens next. It's important to create and meet the expectations of the audience and to satisfy your customer with the deliverable (the next video).

It will be difficult to gain traction and a build a following if you are just posting haphazardly. It is better for you and better for the audience if you make an upload schedule and stick to it. Of course, things will come up at school or at home, and there can be some flexibility here, but it's good to have a basic schedule in place. If you just say, "See you next time!" at the end of the video, what does that mean? When is the next time? Why should I subscribe and make a personal investment in your content if I don't know when you are going to post again?

Jesse's upload schedule changes a bit based on how busy he has been at school or whether he went away with his family on vacation. This is totally fine. He has a few different formats he is working on, so right now, his ideal schedule is:

- Monday – Gaming Video, playing and commentating on a game he enjoys.

- Wednesday – Personal Vlog, anything from a storytime video to a tag video with a friend.

- Friday – Interview with Famous YouTuber. To help launch our **BecomeAYouTuber.TV** business, Jesse has been getting tips from some of the biggest YouTube stars! And as his mentor, I help set these up for him. If you work with me, I can arrange some Skype calls with some YouTubers who will have great insights for your kids.

The organization and commitment required to make this schedule and stick to it are great skills for your kid to master. In fact, if you consider all the different steps that go into making a video from idea to upload, you'll see that these are all transferable skills.

BRAINSTORMING VIDEO IDEAS

Brainstorming taps into kids' creativity, critical thinking, and their ability to see how they can fit in and/or stand out within their community, school, or other organization. Each video should have a clear theme or message. It could be a story from your family's camping trip, or back-to-school tips, or advice on how to be a good friend. Many YouTubers keep a journal with video ideas for down the road. Ideas pop up all the time, but obviously can't be filmed all at once. It helps to keep a running list.

SCRIPTING THE VIDEO/MAKING AN OUTLINE FOR THE VIDEO

This is like preparing for a presentation. Will you script the entire thing? Will you simply have bullet points? Where is the start, middle, and end of your video? What do you want your viewer to get out the video? Your kid's YouTube videos may be just for entertainment, but it still helps to organize your thoughts. I suggest that you encourage your kids to create outlines for their videos. It makes it much easier to edit the video later if it is fleshed out beforehand. The more work done in pre-production, the less work needed in post-production.

FILMING THE VIDEO

The confidence your kid will gain from being on camera is perhaps the best part of all of this. Speaking directly to a camera fosters great public speaking skills. And while they are filming, they are always problem solving – their light will go out, their camera battery will die, oops, they forgot to turn the microphone on, they didn't delete footage off their SD card and the recording stopped. These things happen to every single YouTuber, and helps kids learn to solve issues quickly and move on from them easily.

EDITING THE VIDEO

At first, your kid may make 20-minute videos. Understand that nobody wants to see a 20-minute video from an unknown YouTuber regardless of how cute and charming they are – unless it is a masterpiece of a short film, in which case by all means, please post it and submit to a film festival! But in general, a three- to five-minute video is a great length for beginners. There is so much content on YouTube that NewTubers trying to make a first impression will get more clicks with a short video. Your kid can always make longer videos down the road – and if their heart is in long-form content, they should totally do it, 100 percent! But in general, I would encourage your kids to keep their videos on the shorter side as they start. Learning to self-edit is a skill applicable outside YouTube, too.

Here is the surprising part. When your kid edits their videos, they learn a lot about themselves. Watching yourself, as cringey as it seems at first, is invaluable. You will notice your kid making better eye contact with you, like they do with the camera. They will sit up straighter because they will notice how slouchy they were on camera. They will say "um" less. Watch a video of yourself and notice how many times you say "uh" or "um" – you would correct that, too. They will learn to speak more clearly and concisely. YouTube makes your kid a great public speaker and a captivating conversationalist. Just wait!

UPLOADING THE VIDEO ON YOUTUBE

The actual publishing of each video instills great pride. Your kid has worked hard on their video and now they are excited to share it with the world!

Just uploading teaches a whole bunch of skills:

- Picking a clever and relevant title that will help get views.

- Selecting an eye-catching thumbnail for the video, which is as important as selecting what goes on the cover of a magazine or album. Do the kids know what an album is today? Album, iTunes. You know what I mean!

- Understanding metadata and properly tagging, categorizing, and filling the video description with rich data. (I teach this in the program, but pay attention to what other YouTubers are doing.) Make sure your kid's videos are in the proper category. For Jesse, we put his gaming videos under gaming and his vlogs under People and

Blogs. When I first started working with him, all of his videos were in the wrong category.

PROMOTING THE VIDEO

Ah, the value of tooting your own horn and being your own biggest champion! Your kid has worked hard on the video from Idea to Upload, and they want people to see it! They will become mini-marketing experts as they figure out how best to spread the word about their video. They will tell people to watch, they will tweet, they will Instagram, they will do live streams to drive people to go watch their video. They will do giveaways and shout-outs and cross-promote with other YouTubers.

Does that make you feel better about letting them make videos? Regardless of whether they become YouTube stars or not, the life skills are awesome – this is not a waste of time! And by all means, gently nudge them and ask questions about their process so they know you have taken an interest.

Once the video is uploaded and promoted, it is time to focus on the next one. But wait! There is more to learn! As the comments roll in, there are lots of life lessons to be taught and learned here. Believe me, your kid will have a much thicker skin and a much stronger sense of self after experiencing the YouTube comment section on their videos! They will be resilient! Chapter 8 dives more into dealing with haters and navigating comments.

Also, if your kid is making money, they will become financially literate at a young age. This will help set up a lifelong pattern and understanding of the importance of making money doing something that you love.

Now before you got this book, you probably thought that your kid would just make a video, post it on YouTube, and that would be that. It is not that easy, nor should it be. Just like going after any success in life, there are many calculated steps along the way. Luckily, there are lots of important lessons, too. No matter how your kid's videos turn out, you will be grateful they undertook the process.

Jenn McCallister,
Who Grew Up on YouTube

Jenn is one of the site's brightest stars, and has been creating content her entire life. Here's an interview with her.

How old were you when you started posting videos on YouTube and what inspired you to first hit upload?

I've been making videos ever since I found my parents' old video camera in a chest under our piano. I was about eight years old and extremely shy – except for when it came to being on camera. Making videos was not only a way for me to express myself, but a way for me to *be* and it was a common interest between some of my friends and me. A few years later, in 2007, a friend and I stumbled across YouTube and found that there were other people all over the world who made videos just like us. Seeing others not only do what I love to do, but also sharing it so publicly on the Internet, inspired me to share the content I made too.

Did you have any goals when you started or were you just having fun?

When I first started posting videos online, I was much younger and YouTube was a much different place. At the time, nobody in my small town really knew what YouTube was, and I was only about twelve years old, so posting videos online was just a form of entertainment and expression for me. I had no idea that any opportunities could even arise from it.

Do you remember a shift, and if so, do you recall what it was when you realized things could come out of this? (Do you remember your first sponsored video or a travel opportunity – things like that?)

I first remember a shift in my career online when I went to a YouTube convention in California called VidCon in 2012. Before going to the convention, everything I was doing online felt so intangible, but I quickly realized otherwise after the first day there. I was meeting with brands who wanted to work with me, being interviewed by news outlets, I was even getting recognized by so many people I didn't know for the content I put online – which hadn't really happened to me much before the convention. It was the first time I realized all of this was real.

When did you start making money on YouTube? How many years or videos in? When you got your first paycheck from Google, what did you think? Did you save it or spend it? HA!

I started making money on YouTube around the same time I hit 40,000 subscribers. Back then, you had to apply for something called partnership, which was a program that, if you were accepted, allowed you to put advertisements on your videos and gave your channel a lot more customizability. I honestly applied because I wanted a cool banner, but being able to make money off of my videos was an added bonus. My first paycheck from Google was a little over $100, and I got it in the mail after the first three or four months of being a partner. If you didn't hit $100 in a month, the money would roll over into the next month, so it often took me a couple months to get a paycheck in the beginning – and all of it went right into savings.

What do you think it is about your video that connects so strongly with people? (Note from Buck: Don't be afraid to toot your own horn here! HA! Also, think in terms of comments you see over and over and what your most frequent comments are.)

I think the connecting factor between my audience and me is relateability. I'm just a girl from a small town who spoke her mind and followed her dreams, and I think people like to watch that happen because at the end of the day, I'm just like them. I like to think of my life as an example of how anyone can do anything they desire as long as they put their minds to it.

Did your parents monitor your content and comments early on? Any tips for parents whose kids are just start-ing out? (Feel free to ask your mom this and quote her!)

Since I grew up using the Internet, my parents taught me a lot about staying safe and not giving out too much information even before I started posting videos online. So when I joined YouTube, I was already equipped with a lot of knowledge, which I think eased my parents' minds a bit. Along with that, my parents would watch every video I posted and monitor the comments for a while when I was younger.

What have you learned about yourself through uploading videos on YouTube? What are the life skills you have learned through being a YouTuber?

I've learned so much about myself and life through uploading videos that it's hard to list everything, but I think the two most important things I've learned through the process are how to run a business and how to love myself for exactly who I am. When you post something online, everyone has the ability to comment on or judge that thing. Growing up with an audience who comments on everything, good or bad, was a difficult thing. But through the process, I've realized my perks and my flaws and I've come to terms with loving those perks and flaws exactly the way they are. I wouldn't want it any other way. Not only that, but as you continue to post content online, your image becomes a brand, and I've learned organically through doing everything firsthand how to create and run my own business. Today, the brand that I accidentally created years ago is now a business that I use to sustain myself, and being thrown into it has taught me life skills that I don't think I would've learned in a classroom.

What is your best piece of advice to a young person just creating their channel and starting to make videos?

My best piece of advice to a young person just creating their channel and starting to make videos is the cliché (but always true) "be yourself." It's so important to not fabricate a fake image of yourself and to make content that you want to be making, because otherwise people will see right through it. If you're not doing it honestly or for the right reasons, don't do it at all.

 ## From Jesse: What Your Kid Wants You to Know About Gaining Life Skills from YouTube

I was eight years old when I decided to become a YouTuber. I wasn't happy in school at the time. I had a lot of anxiety and my mom was traveling a lot for work, so at night when I couldn't sleep I would watch YouTube videos by a guy named Stampy Cat. I started watching all of his Minecraft Xbox Series, and it was the only thing that would make me happy when I was really sad. Then I started sharing my favorite Stampy Cat videos with my friends, and soon they introduced me to Markiplier and SSundee. These were my first favorite YouTubers, but really they were my key to being happier.

There were a lot of things I didn't want to talk about. I don't even like writing about it because it was a really hard time for me. But being able to talk to my friends about Stampy, Markiplier, DanTDM, and SSundee gave me something to look forward to. These YouTubers made me happy. And I realized I wanted to do something fun so other people could enjoy it.

School was hard for me. But YouTube was easy and made me happy. If your kid is struggling at school or with friends, YouTube can be a great way to make friends and start setting goals.

For instance, after I set the goal to have my own channel, I started to learn more about making videos and editing them. I learned about different equipment, different types of videos I could create, how to leave comments, and how to follow more YouTubers. This made me feel like I could get good at some things even if I wasn't good at school.

As a parent, you might not know how stressful things can be for kids. Having friends you meet on YouTube who like the same things as you can be really good for kids. It's not just about escaping; it's about feeling good. YouTube gave me confidence to try new things.

CHAPTER 7

YOUTUBE CONFERENCES AND THE IMPORTANCE OF COLLABORATION

MOM! I WANT YOU TO PAY THOUSANDS OF DOLLARS SO I CAN GO MEET MY FAVORITE YOUTUBER!

Uh-oh. Not only did your kid watch lots of videos and start making videos, now they want to go to a YouTube conference. And you know what? You should want to take them.

Now, you may have heard of these events. Some of them include VidCon, Playlist Live, MineCon, StreamCon, VloggerFair, Buffer Festival, Summer in the City (in the United Kingdom!), BeautyCon (if your kid is into beauty videos such as MakeUpByMandy). The list goes on and on and grows each year.

I have been going to these events for a long time. I was at the very first VidCon in the summer of 2010 and have been to every VidCon since. VidCon is like ComicCon for YouTubers. Many of your favorite creators are there to meet fans and network with fellow creators as well as businesses and companies who want to work with them.

For me as a YouTuber, these are the most important events of my calendar year. I live in Connecticut and most of my YouTube friends live in Los Angeles or other areas of the country, so it is important for me to go and network and film collaboration videos. Now, when I go, I will be offering my services as a YouTube Life Coach, which is very exciting to me!

These events also give you a great chance as a parent to talk to Multiple Channel Networks (MCNs) to see if they are a good fit for your kid's channel. There is often a big expo hall where you can talk to reps from MCNs, as well as different merchandising companies and apps designed to help us with our YouTube channels. There is lots of swag and free stuff in the expo halls, so always check those out.

If your kid is going as a fan, their experience will be different than if they are going as a creator or an aspiring creator. If your kid is just a fan and not a creator, that is cool. They will go to meet-and-greets, panels, and Q & As with their favorite stars. All they need to do is wait in line.

I warn you now, Mom: *there is a lot of waiting in line!* You might want to watch some videos before you go – type in

VidCon Meet, Greet Tyler Oakley, Miranda Sings, or Joey Graccefa – and get a taste of the pandemonium that ensues.

Sometimes you will have to wait four to five hours to meet a creator, take a brief photo, or get a signed autograph. For some kids, this is enough. They will scream and cry and tweet the photo and be euphoric for the next few days. Other times, it can be wildly disappointing. Not because the YouTuber was a jerk, but because it's tiring waiting in line, one-on-one time is very short, and kids just get pissed.

You know your kid. Make sure you help them set expectations for this interaction with a YouTube star. I promise that most of the time, YouTube creators are thrilled; pretty much every YouTuber I have met is delightful and adores their fans! This meeting is just as important to them as it is to your kid. They know none of this is possible without your kid watching and being devoted to the channel.

If your kid's favorite creator is doing a Q & A, I encourage you to go. You will get a new appreciation for this person. What may seem like an obnoxious YouTube persona is almost always instead a gentle, humble, everyday human who will disarm you with how much shorter and quieter and cuter they are in person.

If your kid is a fan, your best bet is just buying a Community Pass, which will give you access to community events. But if your kid is a YouTuber who is currently making videos or wants to be making videos, you should definitely consider getting a Creator Pass. This pass gives you access to the Industry Day, typically held the day before the fan events.

There are fantastic panels that address general things such as the state of online video, where it's going, and what's next. There are very specific panels that are aimed at creators to help them grow their business. So many panels are helpful! I suggest you go to the VidCon or Playlist Live website and look for a schedule of events so you can get a taste of what is in store. Oftentimes, the site for the prior year's event is still live, so you can see all the panels that they did.

I also find that the first day, Industry Day, is much less crowded, so your kid is much more likely to stumble into YouTubers and have an informal chat or shoot a quick video. The next two days, YouTube stars have lots of security around them; they're not just hanging out in the lobby of the hotel, so the Industry Day is when you've got a better chance to connect with them as a peer vs. connecting with them as a fan.

Now, you might go to the website, see the price, and think *I am not paying this for a YouTube conference.* I beg you to reconsider. This is an investment – especially if your kid wants to be a YouTuber! For your kid, this is the equivalent of a business trip. I do believe that attending these conferences is one of the best things you can do for them – besides hiring me as their coach! HA!

If you are going mostly as a fan, you can also turn it into a family vacation. VidCon is held in Anaheim, so you can go to Disney World, too! PlayList is in Orlando or DC most years; both are great family vacation spots. When you can tie these events with family vacations, your kid will think you are parent of the year!

The bottom line is that this is money well spent on your child. It's a great bonding experience, too! I love seeing parents with their kids, both of them excited by their shared love of YouTube. Even if you don't love YouTube the way your kid does, the fact that you're reading this book tells me you hope to gain a new appreciation and compassion for their love of it.

Before you go: this is likely your kid's first networking event, so make sure they are prepared. They should have a t-shirt with their user name on it – *they are a walking advertisement for their YouTube channel,* and as they are waiting in line with other kids, they should be talking to the other people waiting with them. If those people are fans, great! They love watching YouTube videos; they should check out yours! If they are fellow creators, perfect! Take out your camera and film a collaboration right there on the spot! There are thousands of kids at home whose parents were not nice enough to take them to the conference; tell your kid that they have a special behind-the-scenes view of this to share! Make sure they are filming!

Here is a script for your kid for when they are waiting in line with other kids at these events:

"Do you make videos?"

If yes – "What kind of videos do you make? Tell me about them!"

If no – "Who do you enjoy watching?" (Keep in mind you might be in line to meet the same YouTuber, so there is already a common bond.)

If they do make videos, tell them about the types of videos you make and say, "Let's make a video together!"

It is best to do it right in the moment. Like a sales call, you don't let them hang up without making the sale. Your kid should not walk away without making a video!

You can do it while you are in line, or during the ample downtime when everyone is just sitting on the floor of the convention center or roaming around the expo hall. Make new friends! Make videos together! YAY! This is a fun and productive trip for your aspiring YouTube star!

Your kid should have business cards with their name, their channel name, their twitter handle, and an email address – but no phone number. A photo of them is good – ideally the photo they use for their YouTube and Twitter profiles. You can have these made very cheaply online. Your kid should be giving these out to everyone! At the last conference I attended, lots of kids stood in line to meet me and handed me their cards. I went home, watched their videos, left a comment, and tweeted them back.

If you are going to wait in line to meet a favorite YouTuber, it is nice if you wear one of their t-shirts so they know you are a big fan. Bring them a small gift or a greeting card that includes your business card. You are being kind – and you are pimping yourself out. It works! And follow up with a tweet to this YouTube star with the photo of the two of you, telling them you hope they like their gift and to check out your videos! Another tip: *wait until the week after the event* to send this tweet. Often times, the YouTuber is busy at their panels or hanging out at the open bar at the event, so give them time to get home and decompress.

The exception: risk a BIG ASK and ask them to make a video with you at the conference! They will probably say no. But they might agree to be in a quick vlog saying hi. If they agree – great, do it! But mostly they say no because they are too busy at the event. The meet-and-greet is like a cattle call, and you really have to just say hi and hug and move to the next person. Also, why would someone with 10 million subscribers collaborate with a fan? They are there to say hi and thank you for watching. That is basically it. But sometimes a determined kid will steal a few moments on camera at these things.

Let me talk to you right now about the importance of collaboration on YouTube. Many big YouTubers grew their channels because they were featured on other YouTubers' channels and got promoted by them. So, you make a video promoting your YouTube friend, and they make a video promoting you. You tell your subscribers to go watch the other video on so-and-so's channel. This is one of the most effective ways YouTubers become successful!

If your kid ends up friends with or related to or dating a huge YouTube star, good for them! They have a fast track, and the famous YouTuber can feature them on their channel and drive their fans to your kid's channel.

Most YouTube stars grow up together on the site. There was my group in 2008, and we all helped promote each other. In 2012, there was a British invasion of stars who came up together.

Your kid needs to meet the other kids they are going to come up on YouTube with. The smartest way your kid can find collaborations at VidCon is to connect with other kids who are trying to grow their following, too. It doesn't matter if one is a gamer (makes Let's Play gaming videos) and one is a pranker (does hidden camera prank videos). Your kid will get their videos exposed to a new crowd via their new friend. If they are both in the same category, that is fine too. There is value in any kind of collaboration!

Ideally you "collab" with people who are at about your same level. If you have 100 subs (subscribers), you find kids who have around 100 subs. If you have 10,000 subs, you collab with people around that level.

I know your kid is going to want to collaborate with someone who has a million subs, but the person with a million subs is gonna feel like your kid just wants to use them to gain subs and your kid has nothing to offer them – whereas when your kid collaborates with kids around the same level, they both have something to offer each other.

When Jesse asks famous YouTubers for interviews, it works because he is not asking them for anything in return. He is not asking them to make a video on their channel or asking them to give him a shout-out. He just wants the content for his channel. That is a good way to go about collaborating with a bigger YouTuber. Ask them if they would be willing to appear on your channel, rather than engage in a two-part collaboration with mutual calls to action.

I hope I have instilled in you the value of conferences and collaboration. Attending one of these events might be your kid's big turning point to go all in, or make them realize they would rather focus on being a fan than a creator! Either way, I hope you continue to nurture both.

Is your kid ready to get started on his or her own YouTube channel? I have a special offer just for my readers – seven free lessons from my BecomeAYouTuber video course, made especially for your child to follow! Just go to **www.becomeayoutuber.tv/readeroffer** to get started.

From Jesse: What Your Kid Wants You to Know About Conferences

Your kid wants to go to YouTube conventions because they want to meet their favorite YouTubers. Also, they want to meet new people and make new friends who like the same things. When you are surrounded by so many other YouTube fans, you can talk to anybody and know you already have something to talk about. Another reason why kids want to go to conferences is that they want to grow their channels and get better at what they do by making new friends, telling them about their channels, and hearing about what other people have. You can also ask your kid if they have something or someone to do a collab with.

You should consider going with your kid because you will get to spend time with them doing something they love. Parents think we only like to interact online and not in real life, but we like to play in person – we just prefer people we have stuff in common with. So if you are sick of seeing us looking at our screens, then come see what we are like offline at a conference. You might even learn more about how to help your kid get better at they do!

When I went to MineCon, I made friends with someone who had a YouTube channel, and he showed me where to meet all the famous YouTubers at the convention. At the same time, my mom made friends with his dad – I made a new friend and so did she. If you go with your kid, you can do the same.

What I liked most about MineCon was meeting all my favorite YouTubers and making new friends. This was the first time I met any YouTuber except one, Evan Era. One of the YouTubers I met was SSundee, and it felt so awesome because I have watched him for a long time and he is one of my favorites. It felt so cool to meet my favorite YouTubers, and I was so grateful at that moment that my mom took me to MineCon.

Meeting my favorite YouTubers makes me feel like someday I can be a famous YouTuber like they are, and that I can have a great YouTube channel like them. I can see how, if I get that many fans, I would go to all the conferences I could and meet all my fans. If anyone sent me fan mail, I would open all of them and mail them back saying thanks.

I am excited to go to VidCon because there will be even more YouTubers I can meet and more people to inter-act with. That's because VidCon is for all videos, not just Minecraft. If my parents didn't take me to conferences like this, I wouldn't feel as confident about my YouTube channel. But now I feel like, "Oh my God, when I grow up I am going to have lots of fans" instead of "Oh my God, it's going to take like 5000 years to get there" because I don't see people in person who have gotten that good on YouTube.

CHAPTER 8

BACK OFF, YOUTUBE HATERS!

Teach your kid how to handle YouTube comments and the importance of safety online.

Let's talk about some general safety on the site to ease your mind!

First of all, according to YouTube policy, children under 13 are not permitted to set up a YouTube account, so it is important that you set it up for them and monitor their usage.

Scroll down to "Policy and Safety" at the bottom of YouTube. There are many great safety tips. There is also a link to the Reporting Tool if you need to report a user for harassment.

Spend a few minutes clicking around in the Safety section and you will feel better and more informed. YouTube wants to make sure everyone on the site has a good experience and works quickly to nip problems in the bud.

Here are my thoughts on safety and what I do to keep myself safe:

- Don't post exteriors of your house. People don't need to know where you live. I actually have a P.O. box in another town for fans who want to send me letters.

- You don't have to use your actual last name. Many YouTubers use fake last names to protect their privacy.

- All YouTubers should be careful about telling people they are going away. I just think it is an invitation for people to break into your house. This goes for parents on Facebook, too.

- Mom, make sure you have access to your kid's accounts at all time. Log in as them to see what they are up to. I set Jesse's Recent Activity to show on his page publically, so his mom and I can see what videos he is watching.

- If your kid is really young, you can put YouTube in restricted mode. At the bottom of the page, it says, "Your Language, Your Location," and right next to that is a way to turn restricted mode on, which will filter out any videos that have been flagged for having adult content. Mostly this is language-related.

So spend a few minutes on the Policy and Safety section on YouTube and put your mind at ease.

Now. Let's talk about YouTube comments. Your kid made a video; they are going to get comments. They want comments! They want feedback! They probably don't really want constructive criticism. They likely just want comments that tell them how amazing and talented they are.

In reality, they might get a lot of mean comments. Some might have to do with their video and the quality of the content. Others might have to do with their physical appearance, which can be very difficult for a kid to have to read.

I made a video with a friend's daughter once and someone commented to say what an ugly face the child had. I, of course, deleted the comment and blocked the user right away. I know my friend's daughter didn't see the comment, and I didn't want her to.

That said, if your kid is serious about making YouTube videos, they are going to have to develop a thick skin very quickly. I have heard of many kids who have been bullied off the site either by strangers or, worse, kids they go to school with, who write mean things on the videos under some pseudonym. Ugh. I am not telling you this to discourage you, put to prepare you for the conversation you should have with your kids about the nature of YouTube comments.

I am so glad that I started making YouTube videos at the age of 31. I had a fully formed opinion of myself, so YouTube comments did not have a huge impact on me. Of course, I loved if someone wrote that my videos were funny or that my videos made their day. But if someone wrote how horrible my videos were, how irrelevant I was, or how ugly my hair was, it had no impact on me. I developed a motto in the beginning that I have stuck to for over 10 years and it has served me well:

"I don't let the praise go to my head and I don't let the hate go to my heart."

Please share this with them. Because if you believe you are as wonderful as strangers are telling you, you then also have to believe that you are as shitty as they are telling you!

So it's best to just accept YouTube comments for what they are. There are many trolls who just find videos and write crappy things on them. Often they are trying to get attention and for people to click on their page. My advice to your kids is not to engage. If someone leaves a comment that is upsetting on any level, you can delete it and block the user. *It is your page! It is your prerogative!*

If someone creates another account in order to come back and ask why you blocked them, know that they are now harassing you and you can report them.

It is important your kids know the difference between a mean-spirited commented and a scary, harassing comment. Here are the kinds of comments you just have to let roll off your back:

- "You suck!"

- "Stop making videos!"

- "Even my dog fell asleep watching you!"

- "What is the point of this stupid video?"

Everyone is a critic! HA! And they may be being a jerk, but this is when you tell your kids the truth. When you put something on the Internet, not everyone is going to like it. Ideally, people will leave nice comments, but things are not always ideal.

I actually used to reply to haters, and I turned a lot of them into fans! Someone would write, "You are not funny at all." I would write back publicly: "I get it. I am new but working on it! Thank you for the feedback. Sincerely, Michael Buckley."

And the world sees this and thinks, oh, this guy is pretty cool and he can handle comments. Maybe his videos are not as terrible as I thought!

You can really make your haters feel bad for being haters, too. I have converted lots of haters who I think posted comments not realizing that I would see them. I think some people think that we just post videos and never look at the page again. It's true that some YouTubers choose not to look at the comments because it helps them stay sane. You and your kid can decide what works for them.

About seven months after I started making videos, someone wrote something like, "This guy is pathetic. He probably lives in his mom's basement and makes these shitty videos."

I replied publicly so everyone could see and wrote: "My mother is actually dead. But when I am praying for her tonight, I will pray for you. Sincerely, Michael Buckley."

Ouch. Yes, my mother is dead, but I am still laughing as I read it because I know the end result. The person who wrote this comment sent me a two-page private email telling me how sorry they were and how they never thought I would see the comment. This person went on to be one of my biggest fans and supporters and sends me gifts to my P.O. box. So my point is, you never know! When you publically reply to haters with grace and dignity, you can attract a whole new fan base of people who appreciate your good nature in the face of crappy Internet comments!

Some YouTubers make videos reading terrible comments, and it's actually very funny. Jimmy Kimmel has celebrities read mean tweets about themselves! Show those videos to your kids if someone writes something mean about them to teach them that even Jennifer Lawrence and Taylor Swift have had mean things written about them on the Internet.

Dealing with YouTube comments is a totally transferable life skill. These are the life lessons you are going to be helping to teach your kid:

- Not everyone is going to like you.

- How to engage or not engage when someone bullies you.

- Not letting other people's opinion of you change your opinion of yourself.

- It's important to stand by your hard work that you believe in.

Now, the above is just for comments that are a little mean, but not threatening. If someone leaves threatening or dangerous comments, you'll want to take it seriously. These are the kinds of comments that should definitely be deleted, with the user blocked and reported to YouTube:

- Threats to your child's physical safety or well-being. REPORT! SCREENSHOT! BLOCK!

- Anything along the lines of a death threat or a creepy sexual comment. REPORT! SCREENSHOT! BLOCK!

- Comments that include private personal information such as home address, school name, or phone number. REPORT! SCREENSHOT! BLOCK!

- Any single user who is repeatedly harassing your child. Someone writes, "You suck, Emma!" on every video, for example. I don't think you need to report them, but do block them. They are just being annoying.

You and your child will learn over time if someone is just being a troll or something feels icky. If the comment section becomes a source of stress, you have two other solutions. One is to turn the comment section off completely.

You've probably seen videos that say, "Comments are disabled for this video." Or you can – and should – moderate all comments. Your kid is probably not getting that many comments just starting out. You can turn on a feature that requires you to see and approve the comments before they get posted underneath the video.

BOOM! EASY! PROBLEM SOLVED! If the comments are what is stressing you out or are a mental block to letting your kid to make videos, do this in the beginning so you feel better about it and less exposed.

Is your kid ready to get started on his or her own YouTube channel? I have a special offer just for my readers – seven free lessons from my BecomeAYouTuber video course, made especially for your child to follow! Just go to **www.becomeayoutuber.tv/readeroffer** to get started.

 ## From Jesse: What Your Kid Wants You to Know About Haters

I have had bad comments from people on my channel. They were really hateful. One person wrote some really nasty words and suggested everyone unsubscribe from my channel. I didn't really know what to do at first, but I remembered that Michael had warned me that this type of thing happens on the Internet. Because I knew it might happen, I felt a bit better knowing I would be able to show my parents and they wouldn't be upset because of some things other people had said just to be mean.

They made me feel upset for a few minutes. It didn't take me long to realize that this was just people saying things to be nasty for the sake of it, and it's not real. It made me read the other comments to see if I could see any bad feelings in those. That actually helped. Because I could see nice comments or funny comments, I felt better right away.

I told my parents really quickly. It was really important that they knew what was being said. They told me exactly what I already knew but needed to hear from them, which was that the person was just being rude, that it wasn't true, and that I should know that there are some people on the Internet who do this for fun. They told me to delete the comment and just forget about it.

I knew my mom and dad were super right. It was my gut feeling, anyway, and my parents basically told me to do exactly what I thought I should do. The person doesn't really mean it. They are just trying to "push your buttons" and make you feel bad for no reason. I felt much better after I had deleted the comment and my parents had talked it over with me.

I'm not scared about getting negative comments anymore. I have a rule. If it's a hate comment, then I just delete it and take no notice of it. My YouTube friends have a great method of dealing with it, too. They reply with a funny comment like, "Hahaha, I hope you enjoyed my video," and if the person writes more bad comments, then they delete them and block them from their channel. It's a great idea, because it gives you some of the control over what appears on your own channel.

Parents need to know that if their kid gets bad comments, they should tell them to ignore and delete the messages. It's not true. Teaching their kid how to deal with the comments is really important, and if they can be there to help the kid feel better when they get a bad comment, then it will be really good. I suppose it helps me to know that my Mom and Dad will be there to help me deal with anything that makes me uncomfortable on my channel.

CONCLUSION

Well, my friends, we have reached the end of our journey together. Or, hopefully, just the beginning!

WHAT HAVE WE LEARNED?

YouTube is not the enemy!

I hope that now that you've read this book, you can better connect with your kid and understand their love of YouTube videos.

I hope you see how simple it is to start!

Just start liking, commenting, and watching to become a part of the YouTube community that is so important to your kid. Join because it is awesome – and also to keep an eye on them. I promise you that the more you click around, the more you'll realize there is lots of outstanding content for you as well, much of which you can enjoy watching as a family.

You have heard my story and you have heard from kids who grew up on the site and have experienced great personal growth and development at a very young age – and their whole life is still ahead of them! I can't wait to see what they do next.

Whether your kid wants to be a YouTube star or not, I hope you feel empowered to help them achieve their dreams.

Remind them (and yourself!) to be patient. They are not going to get a million views overnight, and there are a lot of steps to take until they get to the level of their favorite stars.

YouTube stardom is a heck of a dream to have! I originally wanted to be an actor. I knew I wasn't really a good enough performer to pursue Broadway, but I loved doing community theater my whole life and got so much out it.

It doesn't matter that my dream didn't come true; I created a new dream for myself as I went along. Turns out YouTube was the perfect dream for many of us!

You've learned about different styles of videos, the importance of sticking to a schedule, and not being afraid to take chances. Imagine your kid learning to be fearless at this age! To be so brave as to put a video on the Internet for the whole world to see! What a kickass adult they are going to be if they are this fearless now – I am in awe of these kids!

Your kid is going to learn so many life skills from IDEA TO UPLOAD! After they've spent a few years on the site, you will be amazed at the confidence they exude! They are not just talking to a camera. They are figuring out who they are, how they feel about the world, and what they want out of the world! Yes! All of this comes from making videos!

They will learn the art of self-promotion and become marketing geniuses! They will likely have many ideas for you about how to grow your business and attract new clients! I can definitely help you with that too! HA!

I hope you feel safer and more aware of the features YouTube has in place to protect your child. You know how to prepare them for cyber-bullies. Just watch how they learn how to let things roll off their back offline just as well as they have learned to online.

I hope you go to bed at night and think, *"Thank you, YouTube, for teaching my kids so many lessons."*

I hope my experience working with Angela and Jesse helps you appreciate the benefits of hiring me as your personal YouTube coach. A great gift for your kid would certainly be the **BecomeAYouTuber.TV** training series!

There is a tattoo of the YouTube play button on my wrist to remind me to be grateful for YouTube, too. Oh crap! I just lost you. You think I'm crazy! Listen, it was my first tattoo and I got it to celebrate my 10-year anniversary. I could have just sent flowers to the YouTube office, I guess. I am just an ALL IN person!

My wish for you is that next time we connect you have a YouTube tattoo.

I'm kidding.

But I do hope you have a permanent impression on your brain of how magical and educational YouTube is. I dare you to fall in love with YouTube just like me, your kids, and millions of others all over the world have!

Happy Tubing!
Happy Connecting with your kid!

ACKNOWLEDGEMENTS

Angela Lauria – Thank you for inspiring me in every way. I put you on my vision board a year ago, and it all came true. I wrote my first book, I started my first business with your son, and I am Life Coaching and helping other YouTube parents! Thank you for helping so many of my dreams come true. I look forward to so much more with you!

Jesse Malhotra – Thank you for helping me fall in love with YouTube all over again! It is my honor to be your mentor and my joy to see the eyes of YouTube through the eyes of a 10-year-old! I am so proud of you!

Maggie McReynolds – Thank you for being a wonderful editor and being excited about this book from the beginning!

The Author Incubator – Thank you to Mila, Paul, and all the support team and fellow authors for a great creative process.

YouTube – Thank you for believing in me and making me a content partner back in 2007! It has been a wonderful ride, and I am your great champion!

Lucas Cruikshank, Jenn McCallister, David Devore – Thank you to my peers who agreed to be interviewed for the book. I have felt so loved and supported by this community for a decade. A special thank you to Tyler Oakley for the wonderful introduction.

My YouTube viewers – I am so grateful you have watched me for 10 years! You changed my life in so many ways. I hope you will share this book with someone in your family to help bridge the gap between those of us who understand YouTube is the greatest platform in the world and those who still don't quite "get it."

My family and friends – especially my dad Dennis, my brother Mark, my twin sister Debbie, and all my nieces and nephews and extended family who have always been so happy for me and my successes.

To you the reader – Thank you from the bottom of my heart! I hope you enjoyed the book and can pass on your newfound appreciation of YouTube to your kids! Please reach out to me if you would like me to work with them on building their channel. I'm offering all my readers seven free lessons from my online course, Become A YouTuber. Just go to **BecomeAYouTuber.TV/readeroffer** to take advantage!

ABOUT THE AUTHORS

Michael "Buck" Buckley was one of the first generation of online stars as the award-winning host of the *What the Buck Show* on YouTube. Buck, a well-respected member of the YouTube community, was one of the first YouTube Partners in 2007 and has been a full-time YouTuber since 2008.

He won the YouTube Award for Best Commentary, and the Next New Breakout Web Star of the Year Award, and has been Streamy- and Webby Award-nominated for Best Host. He has hosted long-running online shows for Sony Pictures Television and Iconic TV. In 2012, he won the Live with Kelly co-host contest. He also has done figure skating commentary for Ice Network and NBC Sports.

Buck has appeared on NBC, CBS, ABC, Fox, Fox News, DirectTV, The CW, E!, CNN, and MSNBC discussing his YouTube success, and his story was featured on the front page of the *New York Times,* inspiring many other current YouTube stars.

He believes that no matter what your passion in life, YouTube is the best platform to create and connect.

Buck is also a certified life coach and lives in Connecticut with his dog, who is named after a Beverly Hills 90210 character. He and his 10-year-old "mentee" and co-author, Jesse, have created a YouTube training program for kids ages 8-14 to empower kids to start their own YouTube empires! This is his first book.

Jesse Malhotra is a fifth grader at Janney Elementary School in Washington, DC. He is an avid gamer and loves Minecraft, YouTube, cutting-edge technology, and entrepreneurship for kids. He serves as the Chief Technology Officer for The Author Castle and the co-founder of Become a YouTuber. When he's not in school or on video chat with friends around the world, he is busy building his YouTube channel, MrMalhotra. He splits his time between in McLean, VA and Washington, DC.

THANK YOU

Thank you for taking an interest in your kid's YouTube obsession and for reaching this book! As a special offer to all of you, I'd like to gift you a free trial week of my online course Become A YouTuber!

Just go to **BecomeAYouTuber.TV/readeroffer**

The course takes you through EVERYTHING you need to know to go from no channel and no following to having a successful YouTube channel about whatever you love, and a growing subscriber base!

There are video lessons and examples on how to create your channel, curate content, brainstorm your own content, follow your passion, use metadata correctly, get the right equipment, stick to a schedule, handle videos that go viral, promote your videos, and much, much more!

To start the trial week all you need to do is enter your details – no credit card is required – and you'll get seven free lessons over a week.

Go to **becomeayoutuber.tv/readeroffer** now to get started!

ABOUT DIFFERENCE PRESS

Difference Press offers entrepreneurs, including life coaches, healers, consultants, and community leaders, a comprehensive solution to get their books written, published, and promoted. A boutique-style alternative to self-publishing, Difference Press boasts a fair and easy-to-understand profit structure, low-priced author copies, and author-friendly contract terms. Its founder, Dr. Angela Lauria, has been bringing to life the literary ventures of hundreds of authors-in-transformation since 1994.

LET'S START A MOVEMENT
WITH YOUR MESSAGE

You've seen other people make a difference with a book. Now it's your turn. If you are ready to stop watching and start taking massive action, reach out.

"Yes, I'm ready!"

In a market where hundreds of thousands of books are published every year and are never heard from again, all participants of The Author Incubator have bestsellers that are actively changing lives and making a difference.

"In two years we've created over 250 bestselling books in a row, 90% from first-time authors." We do this by selecting the highest quality and highest potential applicants for our future programs.

Our program doesn't just teach you how to write a book–our team of coaches, developmental editors, copy editors, art directors, and marketing experts incubate you from book idea to published bestseller, ensuring that the book you create can actually make a difference in the world. Then we give you the training you need to use your book to make the difference you want to make in the world, or to create a business out of serving your readers.

If you have life- or world-changing ideas or services, a servant's heart, and the willingness to do what it *really* takes to make a difference in the world with your book, go to **theauthorincubator.com/apply** to complete an application for the program today.

Give Birth a Chance: How to Prepare for an Empowered VBAC

by Ilia Blandina

...But I'm Not Racist!: Tools for Well-Meaning Whites

by Kathy Obear

Pride: You Can't Heal If You're Hiding from Yourself

by Ron Holt

The Face of the Business: Develop Your Signature Style, Step Out from Behind the Curtain and Catapult Your Business on Video

by Rachel Nachmias

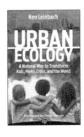

Urban Ecology: A Natural Way to Transform Kids, Parks, Cities, and the World

by Ken Leinbach

Why Can't I Drink Like Everyone Else?: A Step-By-Step Guide to Understanding Why You Drink and Knowing How to Take a Break

by Rachel Hart

Finding Time to Lead: Seven Practices to Unleash Outrageous Potential

by Leslie Peters

Standing Up: From Renegade Professor to Middle-Aged Comic

by Ada Cheng

Flex Mom: The Secrets of Happy Stay-At-Home Moms

by Sara Blanchard

Your First CFO: The Accounting Cure for Small Business Owners

by Pam Prior

Just Tell Me What I Want: How to Find Your Purpose When You Have No Idea What It Is

by Sara Kravitz

From Sidelines to Start Lines: The Frustrated Runner's Guide to Lacing Up for a Lifetime

by Sarah Richardson

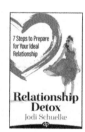

Everyday Medium: 7 Steps to Discover, Develop and Direct Your Sixth Sense

by Marsha Farias

Think Again!: Clearing Away the Brain Fog of Menopause

by Jeanne Andrus

Relationship Detox: 7 Steps to Prepare for Your Ideal Relationship

by Jodi Schuelke

Unclutter Your Spirit: How Your Stuff is a Treasure Map to Your Inner Wisdom

by Sue Rasmussed

Made in the USA
Coppell, TX
05 November 2019